COOKING with
COCONUT

COOKING with
COCONUT

125 RECIPES FOR HEALTHY EATING
DELICIOUS USES FOR EVERY FORM

RAMIN GANESHRAM

PHOTOGRAPHS BY
MATT ARMENDARIZ

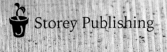
Storey Publishing

ACKNOWLEDGMENTS

Thanks to the following companies for making their coconut products
available to try: King Arthur Flour, Bob's Red Mill, Nature's Way, and Tree of Life.
Special thanks to Vitamix.

The mission of Storey Publishing is to serve our customers by
publishing practical information that encourages
personal independence in harmony with the environment.

EDITED BY Margaret Sutherland and Sarah Guare
ART DIRECTION AND BOOK DESIGN BY Carolyn Eckert
INDEXED BY Christine R. Lindemer, Boston Road Communications

COVER PHOTOGRAPHY BY © Matt Armendariz, except author's photo by © JP Velotti
INTERIOR PHOTOGRAPHY BY © Matt Armendariz, except for those listed on page 277
ILLUSTRATION ON PAGE 18 BY © Edith Rewa Barrett

Storey Publishing
210 MASS MoCA Way
North Adams, MA 01247
storey.com

Printed in China by Toppan Leefung Printing Ltd.
10 9 8 7 6 5 4 3 2 1

Library of Congress Cataloging-in-Publication Data

Names: Ganeshram, Ramin, author.
Title: Cooking with coconut : 125 recipes for healthy
    eating : delicious uses for every form — oil, flour,
    water, milk, cream, sugar, dried, and shredded / by
    Ramin Ganeshram.
Description: North Adams, MA : Storey Publishing,
    [2016] | Includes index.
Identifiers: LCCN 2016030669 (print) | LCCN
    2016038005 (ebook) | ISBN
    9781612126463 (pbk. : alk. paper) | ISBN 9781612126470
    (Ebook)
Subjects: LCSH: Cooking (Coconut) | LCGFT:
    Cookbooks.
Classification: LCC TX814.2.C63 G36 2016 (print) |
    LCC TX814.2.C63 (ebook) |
    DDC 641.6/461—dc23
LC record available at https://lccn.loc.gov/2016030669

contents

introduction

THWACK! THE QUICK RUSH of air from the cutlass, brought down with force and speed, ruffled my hair. It was the only breeze on the inferno-like street in downtown Port of Spain, capital of Trinidad and Tobago — land of my paternal ancestors. The man with the machete grinned and held out the large green coconut he had decapitated for me, making chopping motions around its crown to pierce a hole through which I could sip the water inside.

As I sipped, letting the cool, slightly sweet water slip easily down my throat, the vendor lifted another green coconut — roughly the size of a soccer ball — and went to work again, deftly turning the coconut in his palm as he brought the cutlass down upon its crown (the capped area where the coconut had been attached to the tree). It is a skill that has fascinated and terrified me ever since I first saw my father making short work of a coconut the same way when I was just 5 years old.

A LITTLE COCONUT HISTORY

The coconut, which is native to tropical climates like that of Trinidad, grows on the coconut palm tree, which bears fruit year-round. Its ready availability makes it a staple ingredient in the cuisines of South Asia, the Caribbean, and Southeast Asia, where it is used in rice, curries, and soups as well as sweets.

Coconut was also used, albeit sparingly, in the southern American colonies, arriving as whole mature coconut on trade ships bringing sugar, spices, and slaves from the Caribbean. But it was its wider introduction by Franklin Baker Sr. to the city of Philadelphia in the late nineteenth century that catapulted coconut into the limelight.

> One of these nuts is a meal for a man, both meat and drink.
> — MARCO POLO

Baker's Folly

By the 1890s, Philadelphia had already enjoyed a near two-hundred-year history as a metropolis of gastronomic delights. Food companies had long sought to situate their businesses in the city as a way of giving their products the imprimatur of gourmet quality. Chief among Philadelphia's food manufacturers was a brotherhood of flour millers, large and small, many of whom hailed from families who had plied their trade since the 1700s.

Franklin Baker Sr. was a newcomer to the business when he started his flour milling outfit in 1897. By then, Philadelphia had long yielded its dominance in milling to the great mills cropping up in the American Midwest. But Baker, then 22 years old, was an entrepreneur, so he expanded his small operations overseas in hopes of capturing business from the growing market in Cuba.

For a time things went well. That is, until the day that his ship returned from Cuba not with cash for his flour but with a hold full of fresh coconuts. Bananas or citrus or rum would have been easy to unload, as they were in high demand. Instead, Baker found himself stuck with an unusable product that no one wanted, not even the lone merchant who was known for selling coconuts from his shop in the city. Even he was in the midst of closing up his shop on Arch Street for good.

Unable to unload the strange fruit, Baker made a decision that many would call further folly: he bought the Arch Street coconut works and figured out a method to dry and grate the white-fleshed coconut before the shipment spoiled.

What Mr. Baker did next would change the face of American baked goods — and the future of coconut — forever. He gave away his dried coconut product to home cooks and professional chefs to try out. Within 5 years, his sales of coconut were so strong that he sold his flour business and focused entirely on coconut, relocating the manufacturing plant to bigger facilities in Brooklyn, New York, and, later, Hoboken, New Jersey.

Within 10 years, Baker's Coconut was so universally accepted that coconut layer cake, coconut cream pie, and coconut custard were rapidly becoming classic American desserts — with a particularly strong following in the American South, the one area of the country that had some history with coconut. Now called Baker's Angel Flake Sweetened Coconut, Baker's folly is, today, the recognized standard in dried sweetened coconut for desserts and baking in America and around the world.

The Rise of the Whole Coconut

Even up to the time of my own childhood in the 1970s and 1980s, coconut remained entrenched in the realm of confection — at least for Americans. But in our own New York City home, my father often had a whole dry coconut on the counter or a bowl of freshly grated coconut meat waiting for use. In those days, this was no mean feat — my dad had to trek to the far recesses of West Indian Brooklyn to procure it. Back then, coconut — usually shredded and sweetened — only made cameo appearances in desserts in America. For coconut purists like my father, the sweetened "angel flakes" à la Mr. Baker were not considered "the real thing."

Thanks to my dad, and our family visits to Trinidad, I learned early on that a coconut starts as a large green nut filled with liquid and a thick jelly. As the coconut matures and dries out, the jelly becomes the hard white flesh that my friends back home thought was the sum total of the fruit (if they even knew what real coconut looked like at all). It's only when the green casing is cracked open that the brown shell is revealed, complete with the raffia-like threads that we see on coconuts in the supermarket.

Today coconut is no longer exotic and rare. My specialized knowledge of the fruit I love so well isn't nearly so unusual or strange. Instead, coconut has become a mainstream flavor and, in many cases, a go-to ingredient for healthy eaters who appreciate coconut's nutrient density and low glycemic index, and for foodies who are eager to explore a world full of flavor. While fresh coconut was once a rarity in the supermarket, there is now a great variety of coconut products — from waters to milks, chips, shreds, sugars, oils, molasses, vinegar, flour, and more.

Thanks to its mild, sweet taste, it is easy to incorporate coconut into a variety of dishes to take advantage of its well-touted health benefits. Here I've collected recipes from a number of cultures that have had a long and fruitful relationship with the coconut, highlighting its versatility and easy adaptation to the modern kitchen.

Thanks to its **mild, sweet taste,** it is easy to incorporate coconut into a variety of dishes to take advantage of its well-touted health benefits.

A NUTRITIONAL POWERHOUSE

Long-distance athletes were the first to recognize coconut water as an electrolyte drink because of its high levels of potassium, but cultures with a strong relationship to the fruit have long known that is not all that coconut has to offer. While sweet, coconut has a low glycemic index, meaning that it does not substantially raise blood sugar when consumed — a boon for diabetics or those watching their weight.

COCONUT OIL. While coconut oil does indeed comprise saturated fat, the fat is primarily in the form of medium-chain fatty acids, which are more easily digested by the liver and converted to energy rather than fat stores. As such, they may prove beneficial in promoting heart health. Researchers since the 1930s have observed that people in coconut-consuming cultures tended to have lower rates of obesity, heart disease, and diabetes despite the fat content of this staple food. Numerous modern studies have shown that countries with coconut-heavy diets have the lowest incidence of heart disease, particularly as compared to Americans.

And despite its high saturated fat levels, coconut oil seems to actually promote "good" HDL cholesterol levels, as noted by the Harvard School of Public Health, while promoting the satiety necessary to maintain healthy weight levels. Coconut enjoys the added boon for the health-conscious eater or active exerciser of being real, simple, pure, and natural.

For thousands of years, Ayurvedic practitioners have recommended coconut oil for dental health in the form of "oil pulling," in which pure coconut oil is swished around the mouth to kill bacteria and soothe the gums. Today the practice is widely resurging. Scientists now know that both the lauric and caprylic acids naturally found in coconut oil are powerful antimicrobials that can help alleviate gingivitis and bad breath caused by bacteria. Studies have shown that these antimicrobials are also an effective preventive against candida or yeast infections.

Pure coconut oil is a treasured part of beauty rituals and is massaged into the scalp to alleviate headaches and make hair shine, as well as into the body to make skin supple and ease swelling in the joints. Coconut oil is considered particularly useful for erasing stretch marks as well. In

Numerous modern studies have shown that countries with coconut-heavy diets have the lowest incidence of heart disease.

mass-produced cosmetics, coconut oil is a mild and nonallergenic base for lipsticks, eyeliners, shampoos, and more. As a pure acne treatment, coconut oil is touted for its antimicrobial properties.

COCONUT WATER. If the ancient lore of coconut-producing countries is to be believed, coconut water is good for everything from alleviating nausea in pregnant women to keeping the undernourished alive — and it continues to be used for these purposes throughout India, the Caribbean, and Southeast Asia.

COCONUT FLOUR. Those on gluten-free diets will find naturally gluten-free coconut flour a health powerhouse. While it can't be used in a one-to-one replacement ratio with wheat flour, when combined with oat flour or other gluten-free flours, it provides, taste, texture, and flavor without gluten or high sugar levels.

THE RICH DIVERSITY OF COCONUT

Luckily, everyday supermarkets are stocking an increasing variety of canned, frozen, packaged, and prepared products, and even coconuts with prescored shells, making cooking with coconuts easy. Rest assured that even dyed-in-the-wool coconut connoisseurs use a mixture of both fresh and packaged goods, all of which we will explore in the recipes that follow.

As you make some of these recipes, you will enjoy learning the differences in texture and taste between fresh coconut, dried coconut, and coconut chips, and you will revel in the creaminess of coconut milks and ice creams while marveling at how refined coconut oil — flavorless and not greasy — is the perfect frying medium. You will also delight in the new levels of complexity and flavor your baked goods, smoothies, desserts, and drinks reach with coconut sugar and syrups.

Once the recipes in this book become part of your repertoire, you'll wonder how you ever lived without a full pantry of coconut delights.

cream

milk

sugar

water

shredded

flour

nectar

flakes

raw

oil

1
a coconut primer:
parts, products, and uses

The box grater lived in the back of my parents' kitchen cupboard, behind the pots and pans. It sat tucked next to my father's favorite hand-hammered metal dish that my mother had brought from her native Iran, which he used solely for marinating chicken and meats in his Trinidadian curry powder. Dented and dull, the grater had one purpose: to rend and score the hard white flesh of the coconut that my father would crack open with a sharp machete.

WE WERE MORE ACCUSTOMED to coconut than other folks in our neighborhood. To most, it was an exotic rarity, the stuff of Mounds bars or, occasionally, a Sara Lee cake. But my Caribbean father used coconut in his breads, tarts, and "sugar cakes" — the candies he sometimes made from boiled sugar and coconut — as well as in curries, soups, and stews. My father's baking days only happened a few times a year, but they gave me a taste and a passion for coconut's wonderful flavor, a passion that only grew on visits to his home country of Trinidad. There, coconut is the "vanilla" of the land, the base flavor of cookies, cakes, candy, ice cream, rice pudding, drinks, and a few savory dishes, too. In short: heaven.

My love for coconut remained steadfast and true, even in the face of avowed coconut haters. And, oh, they were many. To them, coconut was an odd artificial flavor, reminiscent of what tanning oil might taste like if they cared to try it. Little did I know when I was a child that coconut would become one of the biggest food trends in decades. Today it has exploded onto the American culinary scene and captured the taste buds and imagination of eaters and cooks everywhere.

The coconut products available today are incredibly varied and diverse. Not only are there numerous types of coconut-based products, but there are also multiple companies offering them. Even the most mainstream American food companies have begun selling coconut products. This chapter provides a primer on each of these products.

THE MANY FORMS OF COCONUT

Coconut is one of the most versatile plants in existence and one from which an astonishing variety of products is manufactured. The fruit, the plant fibers, and the tree sap are all processed and used in multiple ways worldwide. Modern technology has taken that diversity a step further with products that make this tropical fruit not only readily available around the world but ingeniously adapted to modern lifestyles.

green coconuts

Green, Fresh, and Dried Coconut Meat

- **GREEN COCONUT MEAT.** Green coconuts are the nuts that are chopped down from the coconut palm. They are filled with water and a gelatinous substance often referred to as jelly. If allowed to age, the jelly becomes hard, white coconut meat. Green coconut meat is most often scooped out and eaten after the coconut water is drunk. Sometimes, pieces of green coconut are found floating in commercial coconut waters.

- **FRESH COCONUT.** What I am calling "fresh coconut" in this book is the meat of a freshly cracked mature brown coconut. Also referred to as copra, it is the hard, white, aged version of green coconut jelly that is grated and either used immediately or dried further for later use.

- **DRIED COCONUT.** This is meat from a mature brown coconut that has been further dried. It is sold packaged in many forms, including shredded, diced, and flaked, and sweetened or unsweetened. It is historically most familiar to Americans as sweetened flaked coconut for baking.

Shoot

Green outer layer

Hard inner layer

Coconut "meat"

Coconut sponge

Root

Fibrous husk

Coconut Water

Coconut water is the liquid center of the coconut. It is more abundant when the coconut is young or "green" and less so the more mature the coconut gets. The tastiest coconut waters for sale in cans and bottles are from sweet, young coconuts. Mature coconuts do not provide a fresh-tasting water. Powdered coconut waters that can be reconstituted with pure water are increasingly available. In cultures where coconut is prevalent, the water is often used as an electrolytic drink to prevent dehydration.

Most commercial coconut waters are pasteurized to remove any bacteria, although there are a few raw coconut water brands — including Harmless Harvest — that employ pressure treatment to remove micro-contaminants, and these require refrigeration to retain freshness. Raw coconut drinks are more perishable than their aseptically packaged counterparts, so pay attention to the "sell by" or "use by" dates when buying these products, just as you would for animal milk products or fresh juices.

Coconut Milk

Coconut milk is perhaps the most misunderstood product that comes from the coconut. It is not the liquid inside of a coconut, as many believe (that's coconut water), but the coconut "meat" puréed with water into a smooth liquid. The less water used, the thicker and creamier the coconut milk (see description of coconut cream, page 21).

You can easily make coconut milk at home (see the recipe on page 28) with fresh, frozen, or dried unsweetened coconut meat.

It's worth noting that commercial coconut milk comes in several varieties and that, even within a single variety, different manufacturers' products can vary in consistency and taste.

- **CANNED.** The most common form of coconut milk, canned coconut milk is a shelf-stable product that comes in "lite" (reduced-fat) and full-fat varieties. Most canned coconut milk will separate and need to be stirred before use. The most efficient reemulsification method is to pour the entire contents of the can into a bowl and whisk it together. You may also do this in a blender or food processor.

Coconut milk is not the liquid inside of a coconut, as many believe (that's coconut water), but the coconut "meat" puréed with water into a smooth liquid.

- **REFRIGERATED CARTON.** Refrigerated coconut milk cartons fall in the realm of nondairy beverages and can be found next to soy and almond milk in the grocer's cold case. These versions have flavorings and, sometimes, a bit of sweetener. They also contain an emulsifier and/or thickener to more closely approximate the consistency of milk. Generally, vegan seaweed-based carrageenan is used for this purpose. These products should be seen more as a beverage than a cooking product and should be used in the way that dairy beverages are used, with some uses for baking and confectionery.

- **ASEPTIC CARTON.** Aseptic (shelf-stable) coconut milk is becoming more common and comes in two varieties: one is similar to a canned version that comprises only coconut meat and water, and the other is a shelf-stable version of the refrigerated-carton type that usually has flavoring and a thickener or emulsifier such as carrageenan or other gelatin. Use the latter form as you would refrigerated carton coconut milk — mostly as a beverage — and the former as you would canned varieties.

THE TREE OF LIFE

As impressive as the amount of food products that come from the coconut palm are, equally astounding is the multiplicity of uses for the other parts of the tree. The trunk, for instance, is used to make furniture and buildings, as well as canoes, containers, and drums. The roots are used for making dyes, mouthwash, and even toothbrushes. The leaves make bags, baskets, brooms, toys, umbrellas, and much more. Because of this, many ancient coconut-producing cultures considered the palm necessary for survival and sustenance. Often, a young coconut tree is given as a wedding gift to a newly married couple setting up their own home to provide them all they need for a successful future. The coconut palm well earns its title "Tree of Life."

- **POWDERED.** Like powdered cow's milk, powdered coconut milk is widely available in much of the developing world and is becoming increasingly available in the United States and Europe. The product is reconstituted with water to the desired consistency and should be refrigerated after use. The King Arthur Flour Company makes an excellent version.

- **COCONUT CREAM.** Coconut cream is coconut meat that has been processed with very little water. In canned varieties of coconut milk, the cream is what separates and rises to the top. Pure coconut cream is most often sold canned. In the Caribbean and Latin America, coconut cream is sold in a block akin to butter and can be thinned with hot water as needed for the desired consistency.

Coconut Nectar or Molasses

Coconut nectar is made by tapping a coconut palm, much the way a maple tree is tapped for sap to make maple syrup. The sap that runs out of the coconut palm is heated at a low temperature to thicken it. The resulting syrup has a texture that is similar to that of honey or agave syrup. This dark nectar does not have an overtly coconut taste, but it is a sweetener with a low glycemic index.

Coconut Manna

Also called coconut butter or coconut spread, coconut manna is puréed dried unsweetened coconut meat. During the puréeing or grinding process, the coconut releases its natural oils, which allows the coconut meat to be puréed into a thick paste that has the consistency of butter. Coconut manna is used as a spread in place of cow and nut butter and can be sweetened or flavored during the puréeing process as desired. Coconut manna can be made at home, but it requires a high-powered blender like a Vitamix (see the recipe on page 29). Like other butters, coconut manna melts easily and can be used as a liquid application.

Coconut Flour

Coconut flour is made from defatted coconut meat that is dried and ground into flour. It is derived from the solids left over after the process of making coconut milk.

Coconut flour cannot be substituted for all-purpose flour or other grain flours on a 1:1 basis. The main reason for this is that coconut flour absorbs a great deal of liquid. A good rule of thumb is to substitute one-quarter to one-third of the grain flour a recipe calls for with coconut flour and use two to three times the amount of baking powder or yeast if the recipe calls for either. Another good tip is to increase the amount of eggs if the recipe calls for them: generally, six large eggs for 1 cup of coconut flour is about right. When using coconut flour for dredging items for frying, you can simply use it as you would use grain-based flour; however, make sure to sift the flour first, as it can get clumpy.

Coconut Sugar

A popular sugar substitute because of its low glycemic index, coconut sugar is, like coconut nectar, a sap-based product of the coconut tree. The heavy branches that hold the coconut blossoms, later to become mature coconuts, are tapped for the milky white sap they hold. This sap is boiled at a low temperature, past the point necessary to make coconut nectar, until it granulates. Except for the level of heat applied, making coconut sugar from sap is similar to the process of turning cane juice into granulated sugar or making maple sugar out of maple syrup.

When coconut-blossom branches are tapped to make sugar, the process effectively drains the nutrition from the budding coconuts. As a result, you can't have both coconut sap/sugar and mature coconuts from the same tree. Like the coconut itself, coconut sugar is very high in minerals like iron, zinc, potassium, nitrogen, and others, while plain white refined cane and beet sugars have virtually no mineral content.

Like the coconut itself, coconut sugar is very high in minerals like iron, zinc, potassium, nitrogen, and others.

Sprouted Coconut or Coconut Sponge

Rarely seen outside of the countries in which coconut is grown, sprouted coconut is the spongy interior of the coconut after it has dried past the point of having any meat left. The sponge feeds the growth of a new sprout, which will ultimately become another coconut palm. This sponge or sprout is edible and has an intense coconut taste with a spongy or sometimes cotton candy–like texture.

Toddy or *Tadi*

Toddy (also called *tadi*) is the sap of the coconut palm. It can be consumed immediately as a beverage or aged in a process that produces vinegar. Various toddy vinegars are available on the market and can be used in the same way as fruit vinegars: for salads, marinating meats, ceviches, and medicinal purposes.

The sap can also be fermented and distilled into a strong alcoholic drink that, at times, has been banned in the various countries in which it is produced. Toddy liquor production in places like India, for example, is akin to backyard moonshine production in the United States. In the Philippines, coconut liquor is often called "coconut arrak" or "coconut vodka" and is a commercially produced beverage.

STORING COCONUT PRODUCTS

Most coconut products are high in fat, so rancidity can definitely be a problem. A good rule of thumb is to refrigerate any wet or moist product such as coconut milk, coconut water, or shredded coconut meat and to store any dry product such as desiccated coconut, coconut flour, and coconut sugar in an airtight jar. Label the jar with the date and discard any products after 2 months to ensure the freshest taste.

Opening a young Thai coconut

DIY COCONUT PANTRY

For centuries, cultures worldwide have processed coconut into its various forms by hand or by using simple technology. Today, aided by modern kitchen equipment and the abundance of coconut now available, you can easily make many of these products at home.

Cracking a Coconut

Getting to the heart of this wonder fruit takes some finesse — it's no small matter to crack a coconut.

In the hands of those who live in coconut-producing countries, cracking a coconut seems effortless. As a child, I always watched with a combination of awe and horror as my father and his relatives held a coconut in one hand and, using a huge machete in the other hand, hacked around the shell to produce a hole for drinking the water or split the coconut open to eat the meat.

Needless to say, this is not a technique I would recommend trying at home, and clearly many others share my fear of the traditional machete method, as evidenced by the number of new gadgets and tools that are designed to poke straw holes and crack coconuts. For the most part, however, they all achieve the same purpose: puncturing the coconut and splitting it open.

Even without the aid of gadgets, there are a couple of ways to crack coconuts that are somewhat less violent.

POKING A HOLE IN A GREEN COCONUT TO GET ITS WATER. Insert a chef's knife in the tip between the body of the coconut and the small cap at the top to which the stem was attached (shown above is a young Thai coconut, purchased without the green outer layer, but the instructions are the same for green coconuts with the outer layer). Follow the round shape of the coconut as you cut off the cap, exposing the tender beige husk. Use a paring knife to cut a small hole in this husk and work the knife around it the way you would carve a pumpkin, until you have a hole big enough to insert a straw or pour out the coconut water. Make the hole wider if you would like to insert a spoon and scoop out the coconut jelly.

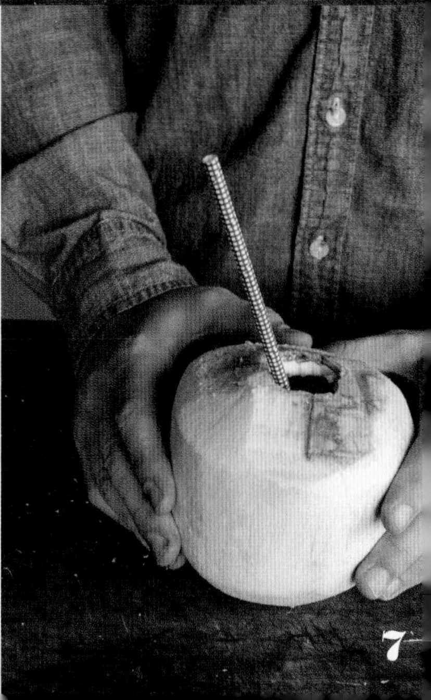

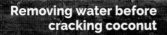

Removing water before cracking coconut

Cleaver method of cracking a mature coconut

RETRIEVING THE WATER FROM A MATURE COCONUT. Before cracking the coconut, puncture the softest of the three "eyes" at the coconut's top with a paring knife and drain the water out into a glass or bowl. In the Caribbean, the water is often drunk with rum or gin.

OPENING A MATURE COCONUT, CLEAVER METHOD. Take a sturdy kitchen cleaver or hammer and, holding the coconut horizontally, tap firmly and completely around its midsection. (It is safest to hold the coconut on a sturdy surface.) Don't hit it hard enough for the blade to go in. Do this several times to create "fissures" from the center out. The coconut will split in half so you can pry out the white flesh using a small paring knife. To do this, work the knife between the coconut meat and the shell and pry it upward. A thin brown skin might come up with the meat, but that's okay. Grate, slice, or purée the coconut meat as needed.

OPENING A MATURE COCONUT, OVEN METHOD. Place the fruit in a 350°F (180°C) oven until the shell cracks and can be easily pried open. This time-consuming (but safe) method can take up to an hour, however.

clockwise from top:
Spicy Coconut-Peanut Dip (page 52),
Tropical Fruit Compote (page 178),
and Coconut Chutney (page 106)

Toasting Coconut

Toasted grated coconut and toasted coconut "chips" are readily available in most markets, and certainly in nearly all health food stores, but it's easy to make your own toasted coconut at home.

1. Preheat the oven to 350°F (180°C).

2. Evenly spread the dry coconut chips, shredded coconut, or sweetened coconut on a baking sheet lined with parchment paper or a silicone sheet. Bake for 5 minutes.

3. Stir well, ensuring that all sides are exposed to the heat, and turn the pan to face the opposite direction. Bake for another 2 to 5 minutes, or until the coconut is just a shade lighter than golden brown. Remove from the oven and allow to cool completely. The final product can be stored in an airtight container for up to 1 month.

Coconut Milk

To make coconut milk at home, you can use the roughly chopped meat of one coconut, 2 cups of frozen shredded coconut meat, or 2 cups of dried unsweetened shredded coconut. You'll also need 1 cup of water for a thick milk or 2 cups for a thinner one.

1. Place the coconut and water in a heavy-duty blender or an industrial food processor. Purée until smooth, 3 to 5 minutes.

2. Strain the mixture into a fine-mesh sieve set over a bowl, pressing down on the solids with a rubber spatula. A nut milk bag is excellent for this purpose. Reserve the remaining pulp. You can dry the pulp by spreading it on a baking sheet, then grind it later into coconut flour (see the method at right).

3. Store the resulting coconut milk in a sealed container in the refrigerator. It will last for 3 to 5 days.

Coconut Chips

Coconut chips are a wonderful addition to granolas and desserts or simply to eat out of hand. Easy to make, they lend themselves well to various seasonings for a unique and nutritious snack. See pages 33 and 34 for flavored coconut chip recipes.

1. Preheat the oven to 375°F (190°C).

2. Use a mandoline or a vegetable peeler to slice thin strips of coconut meat into 2- to 3-inch-long pieces.

3. Spread the coconut slices evenly onto a baking sheet or sheet pan lined with parchment paper, without crowding the pieces. Bake for 5 to 7 minutes if you would like the chips to remain white, or for 10 to 12 minutes, stirring halfway through, for golden-brown chips.

4. Remove the chips from the oven and let cool before storing in an airtight container. The chips may be stored in an airtight container for up to 1 week.

Coconut Manna

You can make coconut manna at home, but it requires the aid of a high-powered blender, like a Vitamix, or it simply won't work. To make it, you'll need 1 pound of dried unsweetened finely grated coconut. Coconut manna can be used as a thickener and sweetener in smoothies or as a sweet spread on bread.

1. Place half of the coconut in the blender and process at the highest setting for about 1 minute.

2. Add the remaining coconut, 1 cup at a time, processing after each addition. Process until fully smooth, another 1 to 1½ minutes. The finished manna will be thick and loose. With the addition of the last cup of coconut, you could also add flavoring, if desired. Some good choices are vanilla extract (½ teaspoon), maple sugar (about ¼ cup), or cinnamon (about 2 teaspoons). Dried, finely grated citrus zest — like lemon, lime, or orange — is also excellent in coconut manna. Add about 1 tablespoon or more to taste.

3. Pour the manna into a mason jar or other container and allow to solidify. Coconut manna will keep for up to 1 month in a tightly sealed jar.

Coconut Flour

If you make coconut milk at home, you can spread the leftover solids on a sheet pan and allow them to dry out in the air or you can dry them in a food dehydrator. Once the coconut is dry, grind it into flour in a food processor or a high-powered or industrial blender (Vitamix, for example, has a grain bowl attachment that is excellent for this purpose). Store in an airtight jar and use within 2 months.

A WORD ON COOKING TIMES

The wide variety of cooktops and ranges in modern kitchens as well as the variation of moisture in coconut products means that the cooking times for the recipes in this book may vary slightly. For best results, carefully follow the doneness cues as the final word on what a step or final recipe result should look like.

openings
(appetizers, snacks, and small plates)

No category of food highlights the diversity of coconut more than appetizers, snacks, and small plates. In part this is because of the strong influence of street food in the many cultures that make regular use of coconut. Handheld bites that are traditionally eaten on the street adapt easily to the Western kitchen and work particularly well transformed into meal openers or cocktail party fare. Check out chapter 7 for beverages to round out a coconut-themed cocktail or appetizer party.

BOURBON-GLAZED
COCO-NUTS

GLUTEN-FREE

PALEO-FRIENDLY

Bourbon pecans in a sweet glaze is a classic and sophisticated snack. Coconut sugar replaces the maple syrup or brown sugar found in traditional versions of this recipe, and finely grated coconut adds another textural dimension. I like to serve these with cocktails, but they also make a great afternoon snack for kids. Don't worry, the alcohol is completely cooked off by the time the nuts are done cooking! MAKES ABOUT 2 CUPS

1 cup bourbon

2 tablespoons unsalted butter

2 tablespoons coconut sugar

¼ teaspoon sea salt

⅛ teaspoon cayenne pepper

½ teaspoon vanilla extract

2 cups pecan halves

¼ cup finely grated fresh coconut

1. Heat the oven to 350°F (180°C). Line a large sheet pan or baking sheet with parchment paper or a silicone pad.

2. Bring the bourbon to a boil in a medium saucepan over high heat, then reduce the heat to medium. Simmer, uncovered, until the bourbon is reduced to ¼ cup, about 12 minutes.

3. Stir in the butter, coconut sugar, salt, cayenne, and vanilla. Cook for another 30 seconds, stirring until the butter melts, then add the pecans and mix well. Remove from the heat.

4. Spread the pecans on the prepared sheet and bake for 8 to 12 minutes, or until shiny and slightly browned.

5. Remove the pan from the oven. Stir in the coconut, mix well, and bake for 1 to 2 minutes longer, or until the coconut begins to brown slightly. Be careful not to let either the nuts or the coconut flakes scorch.

6. Remove the nuts from the oven and allow to cool completely. Store extras in an airtight container for up to 2 weeks.

SPICY COCONUT CHIPS

This sweet and spicy snack is an ideal substitute for chips or nuts at a party or as an anytime snack. The recipe is highly adaptable to your individual taste; feel free to swap out any of the seasonings. For a completely savory chip, omit the maple syrup.   MAKES ABOUT 4 CUPS

1   coconut, cracked and meat removed, or 4 cups packaged coconut chips

1   tablespoon coconut oil, melted

1   tablespoon maple syrup

1   tablespoon sea salt

½   teaspoon ground chipotle chile powder

1. Preheat the oven to 375°F (190°C).

2. If using the meat from a whole coconut, use a mandoline or vegetable peeler to slice the meat into 2- to 3-inch-long strips.

3. Place the coconut in a large bowl and add the coconut oil, maple syrup, salt, and chipotle powder. Toss well.

4. Spread the chips in a single layer on two or three baking sheets or jelly-roll pans. Bake for 7 to 10 minutes, stirring once halfway through, or until they begin to turn light golden brown.

5. Allow to cool completely so the chips crisp up. Store in an airtight container for up to 2 weeks.

HERBED COCONUT CHIPS

GLUTEN-FREE

DAIRY-FREE

PALEO-FRIENDLY

An adaptation of my Spicy Coconut Chips recipe (page 33), this herbaceous chip makes an unusual but tasty addition to a cheese plate or nut mix. It's also great as a side offering with sandwiches. You can change up the herbs for any that you like; just make sure to use dry varieties. Marjoram is a nice substitution, as is sage, but use the latter judiciously because its flavor can be particularly strong.   MAKES ABOUT 4 CUPS

1 coconut, cracked and meat removed, or 4 cups packaged coconut chips

1 tablespoon coconut oil, melted

1 tablespoon sea salt

1 teaspoon freshly cracked black pepper

½ teaspoon finely chopped dried rosemary

½ teaspoon dried thyme

1. Preheat the oven to 375°F (190°C).

2. If using the meat from a whole coconut, use a mandoline or vegetable peeler to slice the meat into 2- to 3-inch-long strips.

3. Place the coconut in a large bowl and add the coconut oil, salt, pepper, rosemary, and thyme. Toss well.

4. Spread the chips in a single layer on two or three baking sheets or jelly-roll pans. Bake for 7 to 10 minutes, stirring once halfway through, or until they begin to turn light golden brown.

5. Allow to cool completely so the chips crisp up. Store in an airtight container for up to 2 weeks.

ALMOND-COCONUT
WHITE BEAN
SPREAD

I love the multiple layers of texture and flavor in this white bean spread, which is reminiscent of hummus but different enough to offer a whole new go-to flavor experience. The almonds and coconut add a greater level of fiber and protein than the beans on their own. This spread is excellent on melba toast rounds, with pita chips, or as the dipping centerpiece of a crudités platter. MAKES 4–6 SERVINGS

1 cup grated fresh or frozen coconut

1 cup blanched, slivered almonds

1 (12-ounce) can white beans, rinsed and drained

5 garlic cloves

1 teaspoon tahini (sesame paste)

1 teaspoon salt

1 teaspoon ground sumac, plus more for garnish

½ teaspoon freshly ground black pepper

¼ cup extra-virgin olive oil, plus more for garnish

Juice of 2 medium lemons (about ¼ cup)

1. Place the coconut, almonds, beans, garlic, tahini, salt, sumac, pepper, olive oil, and lemon juice in a food processor or high-powered blender and process into a smooth paste. You may add water, a tablespoon at a time, as needed to create a paste that is the consistency of hummus.

2. Scrape the dip out of the bowl and transfer to a soup plate or wide bowl and smooth it out evenly. Using the back of a tablespoon, make "wells" in the dip. Drizzle additional olive oil, as desired, into the wells. Sprinkle lightly with additional sumac powder.

SAVORY
COCONUT CRACKERS

The key to these gluten-free crackers is that there is no liquid besides what is provided by the eggs. You can flavor the base recipe however you like by changing the spices or adding 2 or 3 tablespoons of finely shredded cheese — Parmesan is particularly good. Use these crackers with Almond–Coconut White Bean Spread (page 36) or any other topping of your choice. MAKES 15–20 CRACKERS

½ cup coconut flour

½ teaspoon onion powder

¼ teaspoon sea salt

¼ teaspoon freshly ground black pepper

⅛ teaspoon dried parsley

2 eggs, lightly beaten

1. Preheat the oven to 350°F (180°C).

2. Combine the coconut flour, onion powder, salt, pepper, and parsley in a medium bowl and whisk well.

3. Add the eggs to the flour mixture and stir well. Using your hands, form the mixture into a ball. If the mixture is too dry, you may add cold water, a tablespoon at a time, to achieve the consistency of play dough.

4. Place the dough ball on a large piece of parchment paper, then flatten and shape into a rectangle. Place another piece of parchment on top of the dough and, using a rolling pin, roll out the rectangle to about ⅛-inch thickness.

5. Remove the top layer of parchment and use a pizza cutter or very sharp paring knife to score the dough lengthwise and crosswise to get crackers that are roughly 2 inches wide and 2½ inches long.

6. Transfer the scored dough, on its parchment paper, to a baking sheet. Bake the crackers for 15 to 20 minutes, checking halfway to make sure they are not too browned. Remove the crackers when they are evenly and lightly browned.

7. Allow the crackers to cool for 5 minutes, or until they can be comfortably handled, then break apart along the score lines. Store in an airtight container for up to 1 week.

SINIGANG
(FILIPINO SOUR TAMARIND SOUP)

This recipe is an homage to my friend Jason, who challenged me to create a slightly less sour and more flavor-balanced version of this fish soup traditional to his Filipino heritage. For this *sinigang* redux, I've used coconut vinegar and a touch of coconut sugar in addition to the tamarind. I've also substituted the more readily available flounder for the traditional Filipino milkfish; both are in the sole family. MAKES 4–6 SERVINGS

1 cup jasmine rice

2 teaspoons salt

1 small onion, sliced

1 tablespoon grated fresh ginger

1 tablespoon coconut sugar

1 tablespoon tamarind syrup

1 Roma tomato, sliced into ⅛-inch rounds

1 medium daikon radish, peeled and sliced into ½-inch rounds

2 tablespoons coconut vinegar

1 small hot chile, minced

1 tablespoon fish sauce (patis)

2 pounds flounder or tilapia, cut into 2-inch-wide strips

1 cup chopped watercress leaves

1. Wash the rice by placing it in a deep bowl and adding just enough cold water to cover. Swirl the rice around with your hand until the water becomes cloudy. Carefully pour the water into a 4-quart saucepan. Repeat this step four more times, reserving the water in the saucepan each time.

2. Place the rice in a 2-quart saucepan. Add the salt and enough clean, cold water to cover the rice by 1 inch. Bring to a boil, then reduce the heat to medium and cook, uncovered, until all the water is nearly absorbed and "holes" form in the surface, 10 to 12 minutes. Reduce the heat to low and cover. Cook for 15 minutes longer. Fluff the rice and remove from the pan.

3. While the rice is cooking, make the sinigang. Heat the reserved rice water over medium heat and add the onion, ginger, coconut sugar, and tamarind syrup. Bring to a simmer and cook, stirring occasionally, until the sugar and tamarind syrup are totally dissolved, 3 to 5 minutes.

4. Add the tomato, daikon radish, coconut vinegar, chile, and fish sauce, and simmer for 1 to 2 minutes longer so the flavors meld together.

5. Gently add the fish and simmer until cooked through, 8 to 10 minutes. Add the watercress and simmer for 1 to 2 minutes longer. Serve with the prepared jasmine rice.

YOUNG COCONUT SOUP

GLUTEN-FREE

DAIRY-FREE

PALEO-FRIENDLY

Unlike many soups that use coconut milk as a base, this soup uses young, jellylike green coconut meat (available frozen from an Asian grocery store or freshly scraped from green coconuts) and fresh coconut water for a light yet creamy soup that is ideal as a starter for a summer meal. Because the soup is so light, it's a perfect base for fish or shellfish. MAKES 4–6 SERVINGS

1 tablespoon coconut oil

1 tablespoon grated fresh ginger

3 garlic cloves, minced

1 small Thai chile, seeded and minced

2 cups roughly chopped green coconut meat (frozen and defrosted or fresh from 2 green coconuts)

2 cups green coconut water

1 cup chicken stock

1 teaspoon fish sauce

1 tablespoon chopped fresh Thai basil

1 tablespoon chopped fresh cilantro

1 tablespoon chopped fresh lemongrass, white part only, or 1 tablespoon lemon juice plus 1 tablespoon grated lime zest

½ cup water

3 dozen small clams, such as Manila clams, or 1 pound large, shelled, deveined shrimp with tails (see note)

1 teaspoon salt

Freshly ground black pepper

Juice of 1 medium lime (about 1½ tablespoons)

NOTE: *If you choose to use shrimp, add them after you've puréed the soup and cook until they just turn pink, 3 to 5 minutes.*

1. Heat the coconut oil in a large saucepan over medium heat. Add the ginger and garlic and sauté for 1 minute, or until the garlic and ginger become aromatic but not brown.

2. Add the chile and stir well. Fry for 1 minute.

3. Stir in the coconut meat, coconut water, and stock. Bring to a simmer, cover, and simmer for 20 minutes.

4. Add the fish sauce, basil, cilantro, and lemongrass, and simmer for 5 minutes longer.

5. Remove the soup from the heat. Using an immersion blender, blend the soup into a smooth purée. Alternatively, remove the solids with a slotted spoon, place them in a blender or food processor, purée until smooth, and return to the pan.

6. Bring the mixture back to a simmer.

7. Meanwhile, cook the clams: Bring the water to a boil in a large saucepan. Add the clams and cover. Steam the clams until they open, 5 to 10 minutes. Discard any clams that do not open.

8. Add the opened clams to the soup, then stir in the salt, a generous grinding of pepper, and the lime juice. Serve hot.

COCONUT-CRUSTED FRIED EGGPLANT AND TOMATO ROUNDS

This dish will call to mind the American Southern tradition of deep-frying green tomatoes and okra. I like to use eggplant because its meaty texture stands up well to the robust flavor of the coconut crust. The ripe though very firm tomatoes add a slight tang to counter the coconut's sweetness. An excellent starter, this dish would make a good side dish as well.

MAKES 4–6 SERVINGS

eggplant and tomato rounds

- 1 medium Italian eggplant, cut into ¼-inch rounds
  Coarse salt
- ¼ cup Arborio rice
- 1 cup dried unsweetened finely grated coconut
- ½ cup corn flour (masa)
- ½ teaspoon hot paprika
- ½ teaspoon garlic powder
- ½ teaspoon salt
- 1 teaspoon finely chopped fresh thyme
- ½ cup all-purpose flour
- 2 large, firm tomatoes, such as beefsteak, cut into ¼-inch rounds
- 2 eggs
- ½ cup safflower oil, vegetable oil, or canola oil, or more as needed, for frying

dipping sauce

- ¼ cup mayonnaise
- ⅓ cup sour cream
- 1 chipotle chile (canned), minced
- 1 teaspoon freshly squeezed lemon juice
- ½ teaspoon salt

recipe continues on the next page

FRIED EGGPLANT AND TOMATO ROUNDS *continued*

1. Liberally season the eggplant slices with coarse salt on both sides and place on a baking sheet or sheet pan. Allow to sit for 15 to 20 minutes.

2. Meanwhile, prepare the breading: Using a food processor or high-powered blender, grind the Arborio rice into a coarse powder about the consistency of cornmeal. Combine the ground rice with the coconut, corn flour, paprika, garlic powder, salt, and thyme in a medium bowl and whisk together. Set aside.

3. Place the flour in a small bowl. Pat the eggplant slices dry and dredge each in the flour, knocking off most of the excess. Do the same with all the tomato slices.

4. Beat the eggs well in a small bowl. Dredge an eggplant slice in the eggs and then in the breading mixture. Repeat with all the eggplant slices and all the tomato slices. Set aside on a platter.

5. Preheat the oven to 350°F (180°C).

6. Heat a large skillet over medium heat and add 1 inch of oil to the pan. When a pinch of corn flour dropped into the oil bubbles and sizzles, the oil is ready. Gently place the eggplant slices in the pan. Space the slices about ½ inch apart; do not crowd. Fry until golden brown on one side, 3 to 5 minutes, and then turn over and fry until the other side is golden, another 1 to 2 minutes.

7. Remove the eggplant slices and place them on a baking sheet. Bake for 20 minutes, or until they are crispy on the outside and fork-tender inside.

8. Meanwhile, make the dipping sauce: combine the mayonnaise, sour cream, chile, lemon juice, and salt in a small bowl and mix well.

9. While the eggplant is still baking, fry the tomatoes: Add more oil to the skillet, if needed, and heat over medium heat. Add the tomato slices. Space the slices about ½ inch apart; do not crowd. Fry until golden brown on one side, 3 to 4 minutes, and then turn over and fry until the other side is golden, 1 to 2 minutes longer. Set on a platter with the cooked eggplant slices. Serve hot with the dipping sauce.

COCONUT-LIME
CEVICHE

GLUTEN-FREE

DAIRY-FREE

PALEO-FRIENDLY

This recipe calls for red snapper, but use whatever fish appeals to you or whatever is freshest. Ahi (yellowfin) tuna and salmon are often used, and some supermarkets sell sashimi-grade flash-frozen cuts of them. Regardless of the type of fish, it's most important to find the absolute freshest you can, as only the citrus juices and vinegar will "cook" the fish. Serve with Savory Coconut Crackers (page 38). MAKES 4 SERVINGS

1 pound fresh, sushi-grade red snapper fillets

2 teaspoons coarse salt

¾ cup freshly squeezed lime juice

¼ cup coconut vinegar

2 garlic cloves, minced

1 small red onion, thinly sliced

1 jalapeño, thinly sliced

1½ cups coconut milk

Fresh cilantro for garnish

1. Cut the fish into thin slices, with the grain. Place the slices in a large nonreactive bowl or dish and season with the salt. Whisk together the lime juice, coconut vinegar, and garlic in a small bowl, then pour it over the fish.

2. Spread the onion and jalapeño over the top of the fish and cover tightly with plastic wrap. Refrigerate for 15 minutes.

3. Gently pour the lime juice mixture off the fish into another bowl and whisk in the coconut milk. Pour this mixture back over the fish and cover. Refrigerate for another 20 minutes.

4. Arrange the fish in equal portions with the sauce, onion, and jalapeño in small dishes. Serve cold, garnished with the cilantro.

ceviche

Ceviche dishes are common in Latin American countries with coastal regions, and some historians believe they can be traced to Incan societies in Peru. Certainly, today Peru remains well known for its ceviche, but I prefer the Mexican and Central American versions that use coconut milk.

THAI CHICKEN SATAY

GLUTEN-FREE

DAIRY-FREE

PALEO-FRIENDLY

This popular appetizer has transitioned out of traditional Thai eateries into the mainstream. You can find it on chain restaurant menus and in the freezer section in most grocery stores, but it's so easy to make — and you can even create a "light" version by using low-sodium soy sauce and "lite" coconut milk — that there is no need to buy the prepared versions. MAKES 4 SERVINGS

chicken

- 3 tablespoons freshly squeezed lime juice
- 2 tablespoons grapeseed oil, safflower oil, or canola oil
- 1 tablespoon toasted sesame oil
- 2 teaspoons soy sauce
- 2 teaspoons Thai fish sauce (nam pla)
- ½ teaspoon coconut sugar or dark brown sugar
- 1 small red chile, minced
- 1 pound boneless, skinless chicken breast, cut into 1-inch cubes, or 1 pound chicken tenders

peanut sauce

- 2 tablespoons smooth natural peanut butter
- ¼ cup coconut milk

  Juice of 1 small lime (about 1 tablespoon)
- 2 teaspoons soy sauce
- 1 teaspoon coconut sugar or dark brown sugar

1. Put six to eight wooden chicken skewers in a dish of water and set aside to soak.

2. Combine the lime juice, grapeseed oil, sesame oil, soy sauce, fish sauce, coconut sugar, and half of the minced chile in a shallow dish amd whisk together. Add the chicken and turn to coat. Let marinate in the refrigerator for 30 minutes.

3. To make the peanut sauce, whisk together the peanut butter, coconut milk, lime juice, soy sauce, coconut sugar, and the remaining minced chile in a medium bowl until smooth. Set aside.

4. Preheat a grill to high or the oven to broil. Skewer four cubes of chicken or one chicken tender on each wooden skewer. If cooking in the oven, place on a baking sheet or jelly-roll pan and cook for 12 to 15 minutes, or until cooked through and not pink in the middle. If grilling, place the skewers directly on the grill. Cook for 5 minutes, turn, and cook for 5 minutes on the other side, or until the chicken is no longer pink in the middle. Serve warm with the peanut sauce.

COCONUT-MANGO GLAZED
HOT WINGS

Sticky, sweet, and spicy, these wings are wonderful cocktail party food or appetizers. The recipe can be easily doubled or tripled for a bigger crowd, making it a good choice for a Super Bowl party or large picnic. Because the wings are baked rather than fried, they are less greasy. You can make the glaze ahead and store it in the refrigerator for up to 2 days. Reheat it before using. MAKES 4–6 SERVINGS

½ cup all-purpose flour

2 pounds chicken wings and drummettes, patted dry with paper towels

Coarse salt and freshly ground black pepper

1 teaspoon coconut oil

1 small shallot, minced

1 small red chile, seeded and minced

½ teaspoon ground cumin

½ cup coconut nectar

½ cup mango pulp (see note)

¼ teaspoon salt

Zest of 1 orange, grated

½ teaspoon cornstarch

1 teaspoon water

NOTE: *Frozen mango pulp is sold in most Latino and Caribbean markets, but if you can't find it, you can purée fresh or frozen mango chunks in a high-powered blender until smooth.*

1. Preheat the oven to 400°F (200°C).

2. Place the flour in a small bowl. Season the chicken wings liberally with coarse salt and black pepper and dredge lightly in the flour, knocking off any excess.

3. Place the wings on a baking sheet or in a large enough baking dish that they do not crowd each other. Leave ¼ to ½ inch of space around each wing. Spray the wings lightly with cooking spray and bake for 30 minutes, or until they are golden brown.

4. While the wings are baking, make the glaze: Heat the coconut oil in a medium saucepan over medium heat. Add the shallot and cook until just translucent, about 1 minute.

5. Add the chile and cumin and stir well. Cook for 30 seconds, then quickly stir in the coconut nectar and mango. Reduce the heat to medium-low and simmer for 10 minutes. Stir in the salt and orange zest.

6. Mix the cornstarch with the water in a small bowl. The mixture should have the consistency of heavy cream. Stir this into the glaze. Increase the heat and bring to a boil. Once the mixture begins to thicken, in about 30 seconds, reduce the heat to a simmer. Simmer until thick and syrupy, about 1 minute. Remove from the heat.

7. Brush the wings with half of the sauce and bake for another 10 minutes. Transfer the wings to a platter. Drizzle with the remaining glaze. Serve hot.

COCONUT-GINGER
MEATBALLS

These little meatballs combine the warm kick of fresh ginger with the creamy balance of coconut. Roll them small and you have an excellent appetizer. Roll them bigger and serve with soba noodles tossed with toasted sesame oil and minced scallions, with a side of steamed bok choy, and you have a complete meal. You can freeze the raw meatballs; defrost them completely in the refrigerator before cooking. MAKES 4–6 SERVINGS

¼ cup plus 2 teaspoons sesame oil

4 garlic cloves, chopped

4 scallions, minced

1 tablespoon grated fresh ginger

½ teaspoon red pepper flakes, or more if desired

1 tablespoon fish sauce

1 teaspoon cornstarch

1 cup plus 2 tablespoons coconut milk

2 pounds ground turkey or pork

¼ cup coconut oil for frying

½ cup chicken stock

⅛ teaspoon salt

1 kaffir lime leaf or 1 teaspoon grated lime zest

1. Heat a large skillet with 1 teaspoon of the sesame oil over medium heat. Add the garlic and fry until golden brown, about 1 minute. Use a slotted spoon to transfer the browned garlic to a large bowl.

2. Add the scallions, ginger, pepper flakes, fish sauce, cornstarch, 1 teaspoon of the sesame oil, and 2 tablespoons of the coconut milk to the bowl with the garlic and whisk well with a fork. Add the ground turkey and knead well with your hands.

3. Form the mixture into meatballs that are either the size of a walnut for an appetizer or the size of a tangerine for a main course. Chill in the refrigerator for 1 hour or up to overnight (if chilling overnight, cover in plastic wrap).

4. In the same skillet in which you cooked the garlic, heat the remaining ¼ cup sesame oil and the coconut oil over medium heat. Add the meatballs but do not crowd them. Cook in multiple batches if necessary. Brown the meatballs on one side, 3 to 4 minutes for turkey or 6 to 7 minutes for pork, then turn over and brown on the other side, another 3 to 4 minutes for turkey or 6 to 7 minutes for pork. Repeat until all the meatballs are browned.

5. Heat the stock, salt, lime leaf, and remaining 1 cup coconut milk in a medium saucepan or high-sided skillet over high heat. Bring to a boil, then reduce the heat to medium-low and add the meatballs. Simmer until the milk is reduced by two-thirds and thickly coats the meatballs, 5 to 6 minutes. Serve warm.

SUMMER ROLLS

This recipe is a variation on a summer favorite of mine: rice paper wrappers enclosing fresh mint, shrimp, and bean sprouts. Instead of rice wrappers, this version uses coconut wraps, sometimes called "paleo wraps," which are now found at most supermarkets and health food stores and from online purveyors. Or you can make your own using the recipe for crêpes on page 163. Coconut wraps are sturdier than the rice paper versions, and many feature raw ingredients, which provide a bigger nutritional punch. Serve with Spicy Coconut-Peanut Dip (page 52). MAKES 4–6 SERVINGS

2 cups water

1 tablespoon rice wine vinegar

1 pound shrimp, peeled and deveined

8 coconut wraps

3 tablespoons Thai sweet chili sauce

1 bunch fresh mint, leaves only

8 ounces pea shoots

8 ounces carrots, julienned

1. Bring the water in a medium saucepan to a boil over high heat. Add the vinegar and shrimp and poach until the shrimp turn pink, 4 to 5 minutes.

2. Transfer the shrimp to a bowl of ice water to cool. Once cool, pat the shrimp dry, chop them roughly, and set aside.

3. Brush one side of one coconut wrap with sweet chili sauce and layer with one-eighth of the chopped shrimp, then one-eighth of the mint leaves. Top with one-eighth of the pea shoots and carrots. Roll the wrap tightly, then slice in half. Repeat with the remaining wraps until all the ingredients are used.

SPICY
COCONUT-PEANUT DIP

GLUTEN-FREE

DAIRY-FREE

This dip is similar to the satay sauce on page 46, but it has garlic and cayenne pepper to give it a kick. I love to serve this with crudités at a party or as a sauce to go with Chinese dumplings. It's also a very good dipping sauce for the Summer Rolls on page 50.   MAKES ABOUT 1 CUP

2 garlic cloves, minced

½ teaspoon cayenne pepper

3 tablespoons smooth natural peanut butter

½ cup coconut milk

1 tablespoon freshly squeezed lime juice

1 tablespoon rice wine

2 teaspoons soy sauce

1 teaspoon coconut sugar or brown sugar

1 tablespoon finely chopped fresh cilantro

Combine the garlic, cayenne, peanut butter, coconut milk, lime juice, rice wine, soy sauce, and sugar in a food processor or high-powered blender. Purée until smooth. Pour into a bowl and top with the cilantro.

COCONUT PAJEON
(SAVORY KOREAN PANCAKES)

Pajeon are similar to scallion pancakes but can feature a wide variety of vegetables, ground meat, or even shrimp. I like to make mine with a combination of garlic chives, finely shredded kabocha squash, and shrimp. Traditional *pajeon* can be made with rice flour or wheat flour; this version combines coconut flour and rice flour — the latter gives the pancakes a lovely crispy finish.   MAKES 4 PANCAKES

pajeon

- 2 eggs
- ¾ cup cold water, or more as needed
- ¼ cup minced garlic chives
- ¼ cup finely shredded kabocha squash
- ½ teaspoon salt
- ½ cup coconut flour
- ¼ cup rice flour
- ¼ pound peeled raw shrimp, deveined and chopped
- 3 tablespoons coconut oil, or more as needed, for frying

dipping sauce

- ¼ cup soy sauce
- 1 tablespoon brown rice wine vinegar
- 1 teaspoon sesame oil
- 1 garlic clove, minced
- 1 teaspoon coconut sugar
- ¼ teaspoon gochugaru (Korean red pepper flakes) or red pepper flakes
- ¼ teaspoon sesame seeds

1. Using a handheld or stand mixer, beat the eggs on high until they are light and frothy, about 2 minutes. Add the cold water and beat for 30 seconds.

2. Add the chives, squash, and salt, and mix for 10 to 15 seconds.

3. With the mixer on medium-low, add the flours and mix until smooth. The batter should be slightly thinner than waffle batter. Stir in the shrimp and set aside.

4. Line a platter with paper towels. Heat 1 tablespoon of the coconut oil in a nonstick griddle or large nonstick skillet over medium heat. Pour or spoon in about 2 tablespoons of batter, or enough to make a 3- to 4-inch pancake. Repeat without crowding the pancakes in the pan. Fry the pancakes until golden brown on one side, 2 to 3 minutes, then flip over with a spatula and brown on the other side, 1 to 2 minutes. Transfer the cooked pajeon to the platter. Repeat, using the remaining 2 tablespoons coconut oil as necessary, until all the pancakes are cooked.

5. To make the dipping sauce, whisk together the soy sauce, vinegar, sesame oil, garlic, coconut sugar, pepper flakes, and sesame seeds. Serve the hot pajeon with the dipping sauce.

SPICY COCONUT-
VEGETABLE PATTIES

This recipe is a vegetarian version of a traditional Jamaican beef patty. The addition of grated coconut in the filling creates a depth of texture and flavor satisfying enough that you won't miss the meat. The distinctive sunshine-yellow color of the patty comes from being brushed with annatto oil and is a hallmark of this dish, and the tangy flavor of the seeds lends a bit of brightness to the crust. Because these patties can be made ahead and frozen, they are easy to have on hand for an impromptu gathering. MAKES 15-20 PATTIES

dough

- 2 tablespoons coconut oil
- 1 teaspoon annatto seeds
- 2 cups all-purpose flour
- Pinch of coarse or kosher salt
- ¾ cup (1½ sticks) cold unsalted butter, diced
- Ice water, as needed

filling

- ½ slice white bread, crusts removed, ripped into large pieces
- 1½ tablespoons whole milk
- 1 tablespoon coconut oil
- 1 small onion, minced
- 1 garlic clove, minced
- ¼ carrot, finely chopped
- ¼ celery stalk, finely chopped
- ½ cup shredded red cabbage
- ½ cup shredded kabocha or calabaza squash
- 5 green beans, chopped into ¼-inch pieces
- 3 tablespoons dried unsweetened finely grated coconut
- 1 fresh hot red chile (preferably Scotch bonnet), minced
- ½ tomato, finely chopped
- 2 teaspoons curry powder
- 3 sprigs fresh thyme, leaves only
- ¼ cup finely chopped fresh cilantro
- ½ cup water
- Coarse or kosher salt and freshly ground black pepper
- 1 egg beaten with 1 tablespoon cold water

recipe continues on the next page

SPICY COCONUT-VEGETABLE PATTIES *continued*

make the dough

1. Heat the coconut oil in a small skillet over medium-low heat and add the annatto seeds. Stand back well away from the pot or use a spatter screen, as the seeds may pop. Swirl the oil in the pot and fry the seeds until all their color is released into the oil, 1 to 2 minutes. Strain out the seeds and pour the oil into a heatproof bowl. Set aside and allow to cool completely.

2. Combine the flour and salt in a large bowl and cut in the butter with a pastry cutter until the dough reaches the consistency of coarse meal with pea-size pieces. (Alternatively, combine the flour, salt, and butter in a food processor fitted with a dough blade and pulse quickly. Do not overwork the dough.) Using a spoon, stir the dough while adding drops of ice water until the dough just comes together in a ball.

3. Wrap the dough in plastic wrap and flatten to form a disk. Refrigerate for at least 2 hours, or as long as overnight. The dough also may be well wrapped, frozen, and then thawed in the refrigerator for later use.

make the filling

4. Soak the bread pieces in the milk for 1 minute in a small bowl. Remove when the bread is soaked through but before it disintegrates. Set aside.

5. Heat the coconut oil in a large skillet over medium heat. Add the onion and sauté until translucent, 1 to 2 minutes. Add the garlic and cook for 1 minute longer. Stir in the carrot, celery, cabbage, squash, and green beans, and cook until the vegetables are al dente, 3 to 4 minutes. Add the coconut and chile and mix well.

6. Reduce the heat to medium-low and continue cooking for 1 minute, then add the tomato, mix well, and cook for 1 minute. Stir in the curry powder and continue to cook for 1 to 2 minutes. Mix in the thyme and cilantro. Add the water and cook for 3 to 4 minutes or until completely absorbed. Season to taste with salt and black pepper. Remove the pan from the heat and set aside to cool.

7. Squeeze the excess liquid from the milk-soaked bread and add it to the cooled vegetable mixture. Mix well.

assemble the patties

8. Remove the dough from the refrigerator. Dust a work surface and a rolling pin with flour. Roll out the pastry ⅛ inch thick, sprinkling with additional flour as necessary to keep the dough from sticking. Use a pastry brush to dust away any excess flour. Cut circles from the dough using a 5-inch round pastry cutter.

9. Place 1 to 2 tablespoons of the vegetable mixture in the center of each round. Brush the edges of the pastry with the beaten egg and fold over the filling. Use a fork to crimp the edges of each patty closed.

10. Brush the top of each patty with the annatto oil and then with more of the beaten egg. Using your fork, poke a few air vents in the top of each patty.

11. Preheat the oven to 425°F (220°C). Place the patties on an ungreased baking sheet and chill in the refrigerator for 15 minutes so that the butter in the crust becomes firm. When baked, the butter will melt and release steam to create a flaky crust. Bake the patties for 15 to 20 minutes, or until lightly browned. Serve warm.

NOTE: *The patties may be frozen, uncooked, in a well-sealed container or ziplock bag, for up to 2 months. To cook, place the frozen patties in a preheated 425°F (220°C) oven and bake for 30 to 40 minutes, or until golden brown.*

CORN, COCONUT MILK, AND CILANTRO
FRITTERS

I was inspired to create these fritters after eating Mexican-style roasted corn that is garnished with lime juice, culantro (*recao*, an herb in the cilantro family available in Latino and Caribbean markets), and *Cotija* cheese. My version combines all the key ingredients, along with coconut milk, into a deep-fried fritter that can be dipped in a tangy sauce and enjoyed in two bites. MAKES 4–6 SERVINGS

fritters

- 2 ears of corn, blanched in salted water, or 2 cups frozen corn, defrosted
- 1 cup cornmeal
- 2 tablespoons all-purpose flour
- 2 garlic cloves, minced
- 1 shallot, minced
- ½ cup minced red bell pepper
- ¼ cup dried unsweetened finely shredded coconut
- ¼ cup finely chopped fresh culantro (recao) or cilantro
- ½ teaspoon cayenne pepper
- ½ teaspoon salt
- 1 cup coconut milk
- 1 egg
- 1 cup safflower oil, vegetable oil, or canola oil

dipping sauce

- 1 cup crumbled Cotija cheese
- 1 cup buttermilk
  Juice of 1 medium lime (about 1½ tablespoons)
- ¼ cup minced chives
  Freshly ground black pepper

1. If using corn on the cob, remove the kernels from the corn by holding an ear of corn upright on a cutting board. Make sure the wide, flat stem side is against the board. Using a sharp knife, cut from the tip of the cob down to the stem, removing all the kernels. Repeat all the way around the cob until all the kernels are removed. Do the same with the other ear of corn.

2. Place the corn kernels in a large bowl and mix in the cornmeal and flour, followed by the garlic, shallot, bell pepper, coconut, culantro, cayenne, and salt. Add the coconut milk and egg and beat until combined into a smooth, thick batter. Add water in small amounts, if needed, to achieve this batter.

3. Heat the oil in a large skillet over medium heat. Drop the batter into the skillet by the tablespoon, allowing for about ½ inch between fritters. Fry until golden brown on one side, 2 to 3 minutes, then turn over and fry on the other side until golden brown, 2 to 3 minutes longer. Don't crowd the fritters in the pan. Fry the fritters in multiple batches, if needed. Remove the fritters and drain them on a large platter or sheet pan lined with paper towels.

4. To make the dipping sauce, combine the cheese, buttermilk, and lime juice in a small food processor or blender and blend into a smooth, thick sauce. Scrape into a bowl and stir in the chives and the black pepper to taste. Serve the fritters hot, with the sauce on the side.

3
mains

Coconut is ideal for main dishes because its rich flavor profile allows it to stand up to any spice or base ingredient. Coconut milk is particularly useful for sauces and is often the base for Thai curries. Indeed, its flavor is mild enough that it can be used as a substitute in any dish that would normally require cream. As an addition to breading, grated coconut gives fried foods a multidimensional, slightly sweet flavor profile that adds a level of balance to spicy, salty, or sour ingredients. I find that coconut nectar is an ideal glazing ingredient, while coconut sugar is an excellent ingredient to round out rubs for grilled or charred meats.

I encourage you to use coconut products as a substitute for ingredients that would normally call for cream, milk, sugar, syrups, or dry breading. Keep in mind that coconut oil — especially the liquid kind (Nature's Way makes a good organic version that does not solidify) — is the easiest way to get the healthful goodness of coconut into your diet by replacing olive oil or other oils.

TURMERIC-INFUSED
COCONUT
MUSSELS

GLUTEN-FREE

DAIRY-FREE

PALEO-FRIENDLY

Used prodigiously throughout South and Southeast Asia, turmeric has recently been added to the list of superfoods said to cure everything from stomach upset to diabetes to skin conditions. This recipe calls for fresh turmeric, which has a brighter, cleaner flavor than dried ground versions. If you can't find fresh turmeric, you can substitute dried; the taste will be slightly different, but still delicious. Serve 20 to 25 mussels per person, alongside "frites" made from yucca rather than potato (page 144). MAKES 4 SERVINGS

NOTE: *If you're using fresh turmeric, the thin skin is most easily scraped away with a teaspoon, but if the rhizome is young enough, you don't even have to do that.*

When working with mussels, you may have to remove the "beard" from even the cleanest varieties. This is a little patch of seaweed that remains on the spot where the mussel clung to its growing surface, usually a rope of some kind. Simply grab the beard and pull it off. If any mussel has already opened before being cooked, gently press the two halves of the shell together to see if it recloses. If it does not, throw the mussel away — it's dead. Similarly, if any of the mussels fail to open after cooking, discard them immediately.

2 cups coconut milk

1 stalk lemongrass

1 (2-inch) piece fresh turmeric, grated, or ½ teaspoon dried ground turmeric (see note)

1 small red chile

½ cup chopped fresh cilantro

4 pounds mussels, scrubbed (see note)

Juice of 1 medium lime (about 1½ tablespoons)

recipe continues on the next page

COCONUT
MUSSELS

continued

1. Heat the coconut milk in a large deep pot over medium-low heat for 2 minutes.

2. Cut the lemongrass stalk in half lengthwise and, using the back of a chef's knife or a meat tenderizer, gently pound the stalk halves so they are bruised and somewhat mashed. Add these to the coconut milk along with the turmeric and chile and bring to a simmer.

3. Add the cilantro. Turn off the heat and allow the mixture to sit, covered, for 15 minutes.

4. Heat the coconut milk mixture up to a low simmer and add the mussels. Cover the pan and allow the mussels to steam open, 10 to 15 minutes.

5. Remove the mussels and place them on a deep, high-sided platter. Add the lime juice to the coconut broth and stir well. Pour the broth over the mussels.

COCONUT SHRIMP

When it started to make an appearance on casual restaurant menus in the 1990s, coconut shrimp became an instantly popular "exotic" appetizer. Now found on nearly any seafood menu from fast-food to sit-down restaurants, coconut shrimp can truly be called an American dish. I use unsweetened coconut flakes and a touch of coconut sugar in this breading, so it's not too sweet. Coconut–Calamansi Lime Rice (page 135) and a sweet chili sauce, available in most supermarkets, are particularly nice with this dish. MAKES 4 SERVINGS

1 cup unsweetened coconut flakes

1 tablespoon coconut sugar

1 cup plain breadcrumbs

¼ cup cornstarch

1 teaspoon coarse salt

2 eggs

2 tablespoons water

2 pounds jumbo shrimp, shelled and deveined, tail on

1 cup safflower oil or vegetable oil for frying

Sweet chili sauce for dipping

1. Mix together the coconut flakes, coconut sugar, breadcrumbs, cornstarch, and salt in a large bowl. Set aside.

2. Beat the eggs with the water in a small bowl. Set aside.

3. Dip a shrimp in the egg and then dredge in the breading mixture. Place on a platter or tray. Repeat with all the shrimp. Refrigerate for 20 minutes.

4. Heat the oil in a large deep pot or deep skillet over medium heat. When a pinch of flour dropped into the oil sizzles vigorously, the oil is ready.

5. Carefully drop the shrimp into the hot oil, making sure not to crowd them in the pan. Fry until golden brown on both sides, 3 to 5 minutes total. Fry in batches if necessary. Remove the shrimp from the pan and place on a plate or tray lined with paper towels. Serve hot with dipping sauce.

COCONUT FRIED
OYSTERS

I am blessed to live near the oyster-rich waters of Long Island Sound, and so I experiment with any number of oyster dishes. For this dish, you can use any variety of oysters you like. You may find preshucked varieties easier to handle. Some fish markets may even shuck fresh oysters and pack them in a plastic container for you. MAKES 4 SERVINGS

2 dozen oysters, shucked

1 cup coarse cornmeal

2 teaspoons garlic powder

½ teaspoon freshly ground black pepper

¾ cup coconut flour

3 eggs, beaten

1 cup safflower oil or vegetable oil for frying

Dipping sauce (page 43)

1. Remove the oysters from their liquor and set aside. You can reserve the liquor for oyster stew, if you like. Otherwise, discard.

2. Whisk together the cornmeal, garlic powder, and black pepper in a medium bowl and set aside.

3. Place the coconut flour in a small bowl and the eggs in a separate small bowl. Dredge each oyster in the coconut flour, then dip each oyster in the egg twice and then in the cornmeal mixture. Place the breaded oysters on a platter.

4. Heat the safflower oil in a deep skillet over medium heat until a pinch of cornmeal dropped into the oil sizzles and bubbles immediately. Gently drop the oysters one by one into the hot oil. Do not crowd them. Fry until they are lightly brown and bubble to the surface, 1 to 2 minutes per oyster. Fry in batches if necessary.

5. Remove the oysters from the oil with a slotted spoon and place on a plate lined with paper towels. Serve the fried oysters with the dipping sauce.

oystering on long island sound

The original breed of oyster destined to later become the famous Blue Point oyster was first harvested in the wild and brought from Connecticut to Blue Point, Long Island, in the nineteenth century to be farmed. At that time oystering was a thriving industry on both sides of Long Island Sound, with dozens of companies and individuals plying their trade, harvesting wild and farmed oysters for shipping south to New York City and across the nation.

PAN-SEARED HALIBUT
WITH COCONUT SAFFRON CREAM

Inspired by the flavors of India and the Philippines, this versatile dish is perfect for a Sunday supper or to serve to guests. The firm, sweet fish nicely complements the bright saffron cream. Serve this with Coconut–Calamansi Lime Rice (page 135) and Asparagus with Shallots and Shredded Coconut (page 112). MAKES 6 SERVINGS

fish

- 1 teaspoon coarse salt
- 2 teaspoons freshly ground black pepper
- ¼ teaspoon garlic powder
- 2 pounds skinless halibut fillets or other firm white fish fillets, cut into 6 pieces
- ¼ cup all-purpose flour
- 1 tablespoon coconut oil
- 2 ripe plum tomatoes, cut into quarters
- ¼ cup coarsely chopped fresh parsley

sauce

- 1 cup coconut cream
- ⅓ cup water
- 1 (¼-inch) piece fresh ginger
- ¼ teaspoon saffron threads

1. Preheat the oven to 350°F (180°C). Line a sheet pan with parchment paper or aluminum foil.

2. To prepare the fish, mix together the salt, pepper, and garlic powder in a small bowl. Evenly sprinkle the mixture on all sides of the fish fillets. Dredge the fish very lightly in the flour, gently tapping off most of the excess. You should be left with a very fine dusting (don't skip this; it's a crucial step that ensures the fillets won't stick to the pan when searing).

3. Heat the coconut oil in a large nonstick skillet over high heat and then reduce to medium heat after 45 seconds. Gently place the fish fillets in the pan, but do not crowd them. Cook in two batches if necessary. Fry one side of the fish until golden brown, 3 minutes, then gently turn over and brown the other side, 3 minutes longer. Remove the fish from the skillet and place on the prepared sheet pan. Bake for 12 to 15 minutes, or until the fish is firm to the touch.

4. Make the sauce while the fish is cooking: Whisk the coconut cream and water in a small saucepan over medium-low heat until well combined. Add the ginger and saffron and allow the mixture to come to a gentle simmer. Simmer until the sauce is thickened, the ginger becomes aromatic, and the saffron has colored the sauce a deep orange, about 10 minutes. Remove from the heat and discard the ginger.

recipe continues on the next page

5. While the sauce is simmering, prepare the tomatoes: Spray a small nonstick skillet with cooking spray and place over medium heat. Place the tomato wedges in the skillet and cook until seared and blistered on all sides, 5 to 7 minutes. Remove from the heat.

6. Remove the fish from the oven. Gently spoon the saffron cream sauce onto a large platter and arrange the fish slices on top of it in an overlapping pattern. Mound the tomatoes on top of the fish and garnish with the parsley.

MONICA'S KHEEMA REDUX, COCONUT-STYLE

GLUTEN-FREE
DAIRY-FREE
PALEO-FRIENDLY

My good friend, the noted food writer Monica Bhide, served me this popular Indian dish when I visited her at her Virginia home. Based on Monica's original recipe, which first appeared in her gorgeous cookbook *Modern Spice*, mine adds grated fresh coconut to the mix. I find *kheema* can be easily made purely vegan by using textured vegetable protein or vegetable crumbles in place of the meat and reducing the cooking time according to the package directions. MAKES 4 SERVINGS

2 tablespoons coconut oil

4 shallots, minced

1 cup finely chopped cauliflower florets (no larger than ¼-inch pieces)

4 garlic cloves, mashed to a paste

2 teaspoons grated fresh ginger

2 large tomatoes, cored and chopped into small pieces

1 cinnamon stick

½ teaspoon cayenne pepper

½ teaspoon ground cloves

½ teaspoon ground coriander

½ teaspoon ground turmeric

2 pounds ground turkey, lean ground beef, or vegetable crumbles

2 cups fresh or frozen green peas

½ cup grated fresh or frozen coconut

1½ cups chicken stock or vegetable stock, or more as needed

2 teaspoons salt

Plain yogurt for serving (optional)

1. Heat the coconut oil in a large pot over medium heat. Add the shallots and cauliflower and fry until the cauliflower begins to lightly brown, 3 to 5 minutes. Stir in the garlic and ginger and fry for 1 minute longer.

2. Add the tomatoes and reduce the heat to medium-low. Cook until the tomatoes begin to break down and separate from the oil in the pan, 10 to 12 minutes.

3. Add the cinnamon stick and the cayenne, cloves, coriander, and turmeric. Cook, stirring, until the aromas are released from the spices, 30 seconds to 1 minute.

4. Add the meat or vegetable crumbles and cook for 10 to 12 minutes for meat or 5 to 7 minutes for vegetable crumbles, using a spoon to break up any chunks. Stir in the peas and coconut and cook for 3 to 5 minutes longer.

5. Pour in the stock, add the salt, and mix well. Bring to a simmer and cook gently for 10 to 15 minutes if using meat or 5 minutes if using vegetable crumbles. The stock should be totally absorbed. Serve with yogurt if desired.

ULTIMATE VEGAN BURGER

GLUTEN-FREE

DAIRY-FREE

This veggie burger is a great example of what I call a purpose-built vegetarian burger because it's not an attempt to mimic a beef burger. Instead, it's a patty that uses the best combination of ingredients I could devise. Make no mistake: it's got a hefty protein punch, just like a meat burger would, but this time thanks to black beans, quinoa, and oats. Coconut milk and grated fresh coconut help bind the patty together instead of egg, while finely chopped kale adds texture, taste, and nutrients. Serve on a hamburger bun, inside a pita, or as an accompaniment to a salad. MAKES 4–6 BURGERS

¼ cup plus 2 teaspoons olive oil

1 shallot, minced

2 garlic cloves, minced

2 cups finely chopped kale or other leafy green of your choice

1 cup cooked black beans (see note on page 76)

¾ cup cooked gluten-free rolled oats

¾ cup cooked red quinoa

⅔ cup grated fresh or frozen coconut

1 teaspoon ground cumin

½ teaspoon chili powder

½ teaspoon ground coriander

½ teaspoon smoked paprika

1 tablespoon coarse salt

2 tablespoons coconut milk, or more as needed

½ cup cornmeal

Coconut oil for frying

recipe continues on the next page

VEGAN BURGER *continued*

1. Heat the olive oil in a medium skillet over medium-low heat. Add the shallot and garlic and sauté for 1 to 2 minutes. Then add the kale, stir well, and cook until the kale is well softened, 10 to 12 minutes. Remove from the heat and let cool.

2. Add the kale mixture to a food processor along with the black beans, oats, quinoa, and coconut, and pulse until you achieve a coarse paste, 1 to 2 minutes.

3. Scrape the bean mixture into a large bowl and add the cumin, chili powder, coriander, paprika, and salt. Mix well. Add the coconut milk and mix again. You should be able to mold the mixture into a ball without it falling apart. Add more coconut milk, as needed, to achieve this consistency.

4. Divide the mixture into four to six balls and then flatten them into patties about ½ inch thick. Dredge each patty in the cornmeal and set aside.

5. Heat a large skillet over medium-low heat and add enough coconut oil to reach ½ inch up the side of the pan. Gently place the patties in the heated skillet, leaving ½ inch of space around them. Do not crowd the patties. Cook them in batches if you need to.

6. Fry the burgers until they are golden brown, 5 to 6 minutes, then flip and brown the other side, 5 to 6 minutes longer.

NOTE: *I like to cook dried beans for this recipe rather than using canned, mostly because of the texture. To cook any kind of dried beans, first soak them overnight in three times as much water as beans. Drain, then bring the same quantity of water to a boil and add your beans. Allow to simmer until softened, 30 to 40 minutes, depending on the type of bean.*

You can certainly use canned beans in this recipe if you wish — just be careful that the patty isn't too sticky or wet to hold together. If it is, you may need to add a spoonful or two of chickpea flour (or whole-wheat flour if you're not gluten-free) to bind it together.

COCONUT
CHICKEN
CUTLETS

I like to double this recipe and make it at the beginning of the week so I can have it for lunches. This cutlet is great tucked into a sandwich roll or with a side salad. Of course, it's excellent for dinner as well. If you want to make it even more child-friendly, substitute chicken tenders for the chicken cutlets for an easy-to-eat-out-of-hand portion that fits nicely into a lunch box.

MAKES 4 SERVINGS

1 cup Italian-style breadcrumbs

½ cup toasted finely grated coconut

¼ cup grated Parmesan cheese

2 teaspoons dried oregano

2 teaspoons dried parsley

1 teaspoon garlic powder

1 teaspoon paprika

Coarse salt and freshly ground black pepper

2 eggs

2 tablespoons water

2 pounds thinly sliced chicken cutlets or tenders

½ cup olive oil

1. Mix together the breadcrumbs, coconut, Parmesan, oregano, parsley, garlic powder, paprika, 1 teaspoon salt, and 1 teaspoon pepper in a large shallow dish. Set aside.

2. Beat the eggs with the water in a small bowl. Set aside.

3. Generously season the chicken with salt and pepper.

4. Dip the chicken pieces in the egg, then dredge in the breadcrumb mixture and place on a tray. Refrigerate for 1 hour.

5. Heat the olive oil in a large skillet over medium-low heat for 1 minute, then drop a pinch of the breadcrumb mixture in the oil. If it sizzles immediately, the oil is ready.

6. Add the breaded cutlets to the pan, without crowding them. Fry until they are golden brown and firm, 6 to 8 minutes per side. Remove and place on a plate lined with paper towels. Repeat until all the cutlets are cooked, frying in batches if necessary.

BARBECUE CHICKEN
WITH SPICY ORANGE AND COCONUT NECTAR SAUCE

This sweet and sticky barbecue chicken starts with a citrus marinade that helps tenderize and flavor the chicken before it is cooked. The basis of the marinade is Seville orange juice, an extremely bitter juice with a high acid content. While I think the flavor imparted from the smoke of a charcoal or wood grill makes this recipe taste best, it works equally well on a gas grill, or even in the oven. Serve this chicken with corn on the cob, grilled vegetables, or any traditional barbecue fixings.

MAKES 4 SERVINGS

chicken

- 1 (3-pound) chicken, skin on, cut into eighths
- 1 teaspoon coarse salt
- 1 cup Seville orange juice, or ⅓ cup orange juice, ⅓ cup lime juice, and ⅓ cup grapefruit juice
- 1 small onion, grated
- 2 garlic cloves, minced
- 2 teaspoons finely chopped fresh thyme
- 1 teaspoon chili powder
- ¼ teaspoon ground allspice

barbecue sauce

- ½ cup coconut nectar
- ½ cup dark rum
- ¼ cup orange marmalade
- 1 tablespoon tomato paste
  Zest of 1 lemon, grated
- 1 teaspoon salt
- 1 teaspoon freshly ground black pepper

1. Blot the chicken dry with paper towels. Using a sharp knife, score each chicken piece in two or three places. Place the chicken in a large deep bowl and season with the salt.

2. In another bowl, whisk together the orange juice, onion, garlic, thyme, chili powder, and allspice. Pour this mixture over the chicken pieces and cover with plastic wrap. Refrigerate for at least 2 hours, but preferably overnight.

3. To make the barbecue sauce, combine the coconut nectar, rum, marmalade, and tomato paste in a small saucepan over medium heat. Bring the mixture to a simmer and whisk well. Simmer until it is thick enough to coat the back of a spoon, 14 to 15 minutes. Remove from the heat and stir in the lemon zest, salt, and pepper. You will have 1 cup of sauce. The sauce will be syrupy until it cools completely and thickens. Set aside one-fourth of the sauce in a separate bowl.

4. Heat a barbecue grill on high and brush the grill rack lightly with oil. Place the chicken pieces on the grill but not over the direct flame or heat. Cover and allow to cook slowly for 25 to 35 minutes or until a meat thermometer inserted into a leg reaches 165°F (75°C). Alternatively, preheat the oven to 450°F (230°C). Place the chicken in a single layer in a large baking dish and bake for 30 minutes.

5. Brush the chicken with the barbecue sauce in the pan and cook 5 minutes longer. Repeat two more times. Use up all of the sauce for basting, except for what you've set aside.

6. Place the cooked chicken on a platter. Brush with the reserved barbecue sauce before serving.

COCONUT
TIKKA
MASALA

Of all the dishes in the extensive catalog of Indian cuisine, chicken tikka masala has arguably become the best known to the American audience. Ironically not a "traditional" dish, chicken tikka masala was created by an Indian restaurateur in London as a way to meld native North Indian flavors with a cream sauce that would be familiar to English patrons. My version substitutes thick coconut cream for the heavy cream, with the coconut flavor only being a subtle backdrop. Serve with Persian-Style Basmati Rice (page 131).

MAKES 4 SERVINGS

chicken

- 1 (3-pound) chicken, cut into eighths, skin removed from breast, legs, and thighs
- 2 teaspoons garam masala
- 1 teaspoon garlic powder
- 1 teaspoon salt
- 2 tablespoons safflower oil or other flavorless oil
- 2 teaspoons freshly squeezed lemon juice
- ½ teaspoon mashed garlic
- ½ teaspoon mashed fresh ginger
- 1 tablespoon red food coloring (optional)
- 1 cup plain yogurt

sauce

- ½ cup chicken stock, if needed
- 1 tablespoon coconut oil
- ½ teaspoon mashed garlic
- ½ teaspoon mashed fresh ginger
- 1 tablespoon tomato paste
- 2 teaspoons garam masala
- 2 cups coconut cream
- 1 tablespoon dried fenugreek leaves

1. Place the chicken pieces in a large deep bowl and sprinkle with the garam masala, garlic powder, salt, safflower oil, and lemon juice. Mix well so all the pieces are coated. Add the garlic, ginger, and food coloring, if using, and mix well. Cover and refrigerate for 30 minutes.

2. Stir the yogurt into the chicken mixture until all the pieces are coated. Cover with plastic wrap and refrigerate for at least 2 hours, but preferably overnight.

3. Preheat the oven to 400°F (200°C).

4. Place the chicken in an ovenproof dish that is large enough to accommodate all the pieces without touching. Cover with aluminum foil and bake for 25 to 30 minutes, or until cooked through.

5. Pour off the liquid from the chicken dish into a glass measuring cup for the sauce. It should total about ½ cup; use stock as needed to make up the difference.

6. To make the sauce, place a deep saucepan over medium heat. The pot should be large enough to accommodate all of the chicken and 2½ cups of liquid.

7. Add the coconut oil to the heated pot, then add the garlic and ginger. Fry for 30 seconds. Add the tomato paste and cook, stirring constantly with a wooden spoon or a whisk, for 1 minute. Add the garam masala and cook for 30 seconds, stirring constantly.

8. Whisk the ½ cup cooking liquid from the chicken into the pot. Mix until fully incorporated. Whisk in the coconut cream until the mixture is smooth.

9. Using tongs, add the chicken pieces to the sauce. Bring to a simmer and cook gently over medium-low heat for 10 minutes.

10. Rub the fenugreek leaves together between your palms and add them to the pot. Simmer 1 minute longer.

COCONUT–SALSA VERDE
BURRITOS

I created this recipe for my daughter, who loves a certain brand of frozen salsa verde burritos with roasted serrano chiles and tomatillos. I use coconut milk to add extra creaminess to the sauce. If you are not dairy-free, you can sprinkle the burritos with *queso blanco* or other mild Mexican cheese before baking. MAKES 4 SERVINGS

6 medium tomatillos, outer husk peeled

1 small onion, peeled

3 garlic cloves, peeled

3 serrano chiles

1 teaspoon safflower oil or vegetable oil

2 pounds boneless, skinless chicken breast, cut into ½-inch cubes

1 tablespoon finely chopped fresh cilantro

1 teaspoon dried oregano

½ teaspoon ground cumin

½ cup coconut milk

1 teaspoon salt

8 large tortillas

Diced tomato, onion, and avocado for garnish

Finely chopped fresh cilantro for garnish (optional)

1. Preheat the oven to 450°F (230°C).

2. Place the tomatillos, onion, garlic, and chiles on a baking sheet. Bake for 20 to 25 minutes, or until they begin to blacken and blister. Let cool on a wire rack.

3. Remove the chile stems and slice the chiles in half. Gently scrape out the seeds.

4. Place the tomatillos, onion, garlic, and chiles in a food processor and pulse to a thick paste. Set aside.

5. Heat the safflower oil in a large deep skillet over medium heat for 1 minute, then add the chicken. Sauté until the chicken begins to lightly brown, 12 or 15 minutes.

6. Add the tomatillo paste to the skillet and mix well. Fry for 2 to 3 minutes, then stir in the cilantro, oregano, and cumin. Cook for 1 minute longer.

7. Stir in the coconut milk and salt and reduce the heat to low. Simmer, stirring occasionally, until the sauce is thick, 10 to 15 minutes. Remove from the heat.

recipe continues on page 84

COCONUT–SALSA VERDE BURRITOS

continued

8. Spoon about ⅔ cup of the chicken mixture into the lower third of a tortilla. Fold the tortilla up and over the mixture but do not bring one side of the tortilla to meet the other yet. Fold the sides of the tortilla in toward the middle, over the mound of filling. Continue to roll the first fold. Arrange in a baking dish that has been lightly sprayed with cooking spray. Repeat with all the filling and tortillas.

9. Bake for 5 to 7 minutes, or until the tortillas begin to lightly brown in spots. Serve garnished with diced tomato, onion, and avocado and the cilantro, if using.

BRAZILIAN-STYLE
COCONUT-CASHEW CHICKEN
(XIM XIM DE GALINHA)

Full disclosure: With its deep rich sauce and nuanced flavors, *xim xim de galinha* is one of my favorite chicken stews. The *dendê* (palm oil) and dried shrimp may be difficult to source but should be available in South American markets. You can substitute regular safflower oil for the *dendê* and fresh small shrimp for the dried, which will create a different though still complex and delicious end result. Because you'll need to marinate the chicken for at least 2 hours, this is a perfect do-ahead dish. Serve with white rice and hot sauce, if desired.   MAKES 4–6 SERVINGS

- 1 (3-pound) chicken, cut into eighths and skinned (leave skin on wing pieces), or 3 pounds skinless bone-in chicken breasts and thighs
- 2 medium limes, juiced (about 3 tablespoons), peels reserved
- 1 tablespoon salt
- 2 large bunches scallions, roughly chopped
- ⅓ cup roasted cashews
- ⅓ cup roasted peanuts
- 2 garlic cloves

- 1 cup loosely packed chopped fresh culantro (recao) or cilantro, plus additional chopped herb for garnish
- 1 tablespoon chopped fresh parsley
- 1 tablespoon finely grated fresh ginger
- 1 malagueta chile or small Thai chile, seeded
- 1 cup peeled dried shrimp
- 2⅓ cups water, or more as needed
- ⅓ cup dendê (palm oil)
- ¼ cup safflower oil
- 2 cups coconut milk

recipe continues on the next page

COCONUT-CASHEW CHICKEN

continued

1. Place the chicken pieces in a large deep bowl and add the lime juice and salt. Using the lime peels like scrubbers, rub the salt into the chicken pieces. Drop the lime peels into the bowl and mix well. Add enough cold water to cover the chicken and lime peels, then cover the bowl with plastic wrap. Refrigerate while you prepare the rest of the ingredients.

2. Combine the scallions, cashews, peanuts, garlic, culantro, parsley, ginger, and chile in a food processor or blender. Process to a rough paste, about 30 to 40 seconds. Add half of the dried shrimp and process another 30 seconds. Add ⅓ cup of the water to the mixture and continue to process into a smooth paste. Add more water as needed to achieve a smooth consistency.

3. Remove the chicken from the refrigerator and drain. Discard the lime peels. Pat the chicken pieces dry and return them to the bowl, along with the seasoning paste. Massage the paste into the chicken and cover again with plastic wrap. Refrigerate for 2 hours and up to overnight.

4. Combine the remaining dried shrimp with half of the dendê oil in a small bowl. Cover with plastic wrap and set aside.

5. When the chicken is done marinating, heat the safflower oil in a large pan over medium heat. Place the chicken pieces in the pan in a single layer. Do not crowd the pieces. Brown the chicken on all sides, about 5 to 6 minutes per side.

6. Scrape any remaining marinade from the chicken bowl into the pan. Add the remaining 2 cups water and the shrimp-dendê mixture. Bring to a simmer and cook gently for 20 minutes.

7. Stir in the coconut milk and simmer for 25 to 30 minutes. Stir in the remaining dendê and simmer for 2 to 3 minutes longer. Garnish with chopped culantro.

flavors of bahia

Traditional to the Brazilian state of Bahia, this dish of chicken marinated in an herb paste and stewed in cashews and coconut milk makes use of African palm oil (*dendê*) and malagueta chile, which originated in Mozambique, along with the dried shrimp common in Brazilian cooking.

CHICKEN KORMA

GLUTEN-FREE

DAIRY-FREE

Chicken korma is a well-known Indian restaurant dish that is beloved for its saucy richness achieved with a mixture of coconut milk and almond butter. For those avoiding dairy products, it is an ideal way to enjoy a deliciously creamy repast. This dish is easily made not only vegetarian but vegan by substituting a variety of seasonal vegetables for the chicken. Look for that variation on page 128. Serve with Persian-Style Basmati Rice (page 131). MAKES 4 SERVINGS

3 pounds boneless, skinless chicken thighs, cut into 1-inch cubes

1 tablespoon garam masala

2 tablespoons safflower oil

1 small onion, thinly sliced

2 garlic cloves, minced

1 tablespoon grated fresh ginger

1 small dried chile

1 teaspoon ground turmeric

3 green cardamom pods, crushed slightly

1 teaspoon salt

1½ cups water

3 tablespoons almond butter

2 cups coconut milk

1. Combine the chicken pieces and the garam masala in a large bowl and mix well. Cover with plastic wrap and refrigerate for 1 hour.

2. Heat the safflower oil in a large saucepan over medium heat. Add the onion and fry until the onion begins to soften, 2 to 3 minutes.

3. Add the garlic and ginger and fry, stirring constantly, until just fragrant, about 1 minute. Add the chile, turmeric, and cardamom, and fry for 1 minute longer, stirring constantly.

4. Add the chicken pieces to the pan and mix well. Fry until the pieces begin to brown on all sides, 7 to 8 minutes. Add the salt and mix well.

5. Stir in the water. Bring to a simmer and cook gently until the water reduces by half, 10 to 15 minutes.

6. Stir in the almond butter and mix well. Simmer for 2 minutes so that the almond butter breaks up and you have smooth, thick sauce.

7. Stir in the coconut milk and mix well. Simmer for 10 minutes longer. The sauce should be thick and creamy and pale yellow or beige in color.

COCONUT-CASHEW
FRIED CHICKEN

Who doesn't love fried chicken? There are versions of fried chicken the world over. My version uses highly seasoned finely ground coconut and cashew for an extra-crispy golden crust. Serve with your favorite potato salad, biscuits, greens, or corn on the cob. MAKES 4 SERVINGS

1 (3-pound) chicken, cut into eighths, or 3 pounds bone-in breasts, thighs, and legs

Salt and freshly ground black pepper

2 teaspoons garlic powder

2 cups buttermilk

¾ cup coconut flour

½ cup salted cashews

1 teaspoon red pepper flakes

½ cup coarse cornmeal

1 teaspoon onion powder

½ teaspoon ground cumin

2 cups vegetable oil for frying

1. Blot the chicken dry with paper towels and place in a large shallow bowl. Season liberally with salt and pepper. Sprinkle with 1 teaspoon of the garlic powder and cover with the buttermilk. Refrigerate for at least a couple of hours, but preferably overnight.

2. Combine the coconut flour, cashews, and red pepper flakes in a food processor and process to a fine powder. Scrape the mixture into a large shallow bowl. Add the cornmeal, onion powder, cumin, and the remaining 1 teaspoon garlic powder. Mix well.

3. Remove the chicken from the refrigerator. Take out one piece of chicken and shake off most of the buttermilk. Dredge the piece in the breading mixture and place on a platter or sheet pan lined with parchment paper. Repeat with the remaining chicken. Refrigerate for 2 hours, uncovered (this helps create a crunchy crust that doesn't absorb too much oil).

4. Preheat the oven to 400°F (200°C).

5. Heat the vegetable oil in a large deep skillet or cast-iron pot over medium-low heat. When a pinch of flour dropped into the oil sizzles immediately, the oil is ready.

6. Add the chicken pieces to the pan without crowding them. Fry the chicken pieces until golden brown, 7 to 8 minutes per side. Remove the chicken and place on a baking sheet or sheet pan. Repeat until all the chicken pieces are fried.

7. Bake the fried chicken for 15 to 20 minutes, or until cooked through. Serve hot.

COCONUT
SPARERIBS

This is my version of Chinese spareribs that a friend taught me long ago. The recipe traditionally calls for honey, but I use coconut nectar and up the amount of ginger and garlic because I happen to like both of those ingredients a great deal. I suggest you cook the ribs as a whole rack and slice them apart only after they are finished. These are particularly good with Jamaican Bammy Cakes (page 140). MAKES 4 SERVINGS

1 cup Chinese rice wine

½ cup soy sauce

6 garlic cloves, minced

2 tablespoons grated fresh ginger

½ cup coconut nectar

¼ cup hoisin sauce

1 tablespoon Chinese five-spice powder

Freshly ground white pepper

2 racks St. Louis–style spareribs

Salt

1. Whisk together the rice wine, soy sauce, garlic, and ginger in a large bowl. Set aside to marinate for 10 minutes.

2. Add the coconut nectar and hoisin sauce, whisking until they are completely dissolved. Add the five-spice powder and 1 teaspoon white pepper, and whisk to ensure all the ingredients are well combined.

3. Rinse the spareribs in cold water and pat dry with paper towels. Season generously with salt and white pepper, then place in a container that is large enough to hold the marinade and the ribs in a single layer.

4. Pour the marinade over the ribs and cover with plastic wrap. Marinate in the refrigerator overnight.

5. If cooking the ribs on a grill, heat the grill on medium-high and lightly brush the grill rack with oil. Place the ribs on the grill, away from the direct flame, and cover. Cook, turning once or twice, until the ribs are deeply browned and firm to the touch, 30 to 35 minutes. Brush with marinade several times during the cooking. If cooking the ribs in the oven, preheat the oven to 325°F (165°C). Place the ribs on a lightly greased broiling tray or sheet pan with sides. Roast for 40 to 50 minutes, basting with marinade 2 or 3 times, or until tender and cooked through.

6. To serve the ribs, allow them to cool for 5 minutes and then, using a sharp knife, cut between each rib bone to separate them.

COCONUT
PORK
KEBABS

The secret to these kebabs is marinating the pork cubes for at least 2 hours and preferably overnight. Serve them with grilled vegetables and any of the rice dishes in this book, Jeweled Couscous (page 137), or Jamaican Bammy Cakes (page 140). You will need four metal skewers or wooden skewers soaked in water. MAKES 4 SERVINGS

pork with marinade

½ cup coconut vinegar

2 garlic cloves, minced

1 small shallot, minced

1 teaspoon freshly ground black pepper

1 teaspoon salt

1 teaspoon ground cumin

2 pounds boneless pork shoulder, cut into 1-inch cubes

basting oil

¼ cup coconut oil

2 teaspoons smoked paprika

1 teaspoon minced Thai chile

2 tablespoons finely chopped fresh cilantro

kebabs

12–16 cherry tomatoes

2 small onions, peeled and quartered

1 medium zucchini, cut into 1-inch chunks

2 large red bell peppers, seeded and cut into 2-inch pieces

1. To make the pork marinade, whisk together the coconut vinegar, garlic, shallot, black pepper, salt, and cumin in a large deep bowl. Add the pork and cover with plastic wrap. Refrigerate for at least 2 hours, but preferably overnight.

2. To make the basting oil, combine the coconut oil, smoked paprika, chile, and cilantro in a small bowl. Set aside.

3. To make the kebabs, place a piece of pork onto a metal skewer or a wooden skewer soaked in water. Add a tomato, then another piece of pork. Follow with a piece of onion, another piece of pork, a chunk of zucchini, another piece of pork, and a piece of red pepper. Repeat so there are 5 to 6 pieces of pork in all, along with vegetables, on the skewer. Repeat for the remaining three skewers.

4. Heat a grill to medium-high and brush the grill rack with oil. Grill the kebabs for 10 to 12 minutes. Brush each kebab top to bottom with the basting oil and cook for 1 to 3 minutes. Flip the kebab skewers and coat the other side with basting oil. Cook the kebabs, continuing to baste until all of the oil is used up, until the pork is cooked through, 3 to 5 minutes longer.

5. Remove the kebabs from the grill and allow them to cool slightly before serving.

SPICY COCONUT
PUMPKIN
SOUP

This Caribbean-style pumpkin soup is one of my favorite soups to make in the fall when squashes and pumpkins are most readily available. If you can't find calabaza (West Indian pumpkin) in a Caribbean or Indian market, use butternut squash, Japanese kabocha squash, or Cinderella pumpkin (a.k.a. Long Island cheese pumpkin). Serve this soup with a good crusty bread or a salad of hearty greens for an autumn lunch. MAKES 4–6 SERVINGS

- 2 tablespoons coconut oil
- 1 pound calabaza pumpkin, seeded, peeled, and cut into chunks
- 1 small onion, minced
- 3 garlic cloves, minced
- 1 ají dulce pepper, seeded and minced
- 1 teaspoon dark brown sugar
- ½ teaspoon ground cumin
- 2 cups coconut milk
- 1 cup chicken broth or vegetable broth
  Salt and freshly ground black pepper
- 2 tablespoons chopped fresh cilantro

1. Heat the coconut oil in a large saucepan over medium heat. Add the pumpkin, stir well, and cook, covered, for 15 minutes.

2. Add the onion, garlic, and ají dulce and stir well. Sauté until the onion becomes translucent, 3 to 5 minutes, then add the brown sugar and cumin. Mix well. Cook until the sugar melts, 2 to 3 minutes.

3. Stir in the coconut milk and broth. Bring to a simmer and cook, uncovered, until the pumpkin is very soft, about 15 minutes.

4. Using an immersion blender, blend the soup into a smooth purée. Alternatively, remove the solids with a slotted spoon and place in a blender or food processor. Purée until smooth and return to the pan.

5. Bring back to a simmer and cook gently for 5 minutes so the flavors combine. Season with salt and black pepper to taste. Serve hot, garnished with the cilantro.

THAI COCONUT
CHICKEN
SOUP

GLUTEN-FREE

DAIRY-FREE

PALEO-FRIENDLY

This is my version of the classic soup found in Thai restaurants. The amount of coconut milk is absolutely necessary for creating a thick, white soup that can be a meal in itself, paired with a light salad. Feel free to adjust the fish sauce to taste, as it can be an intense and salty flavor. You can find fresh lemongrass and kaffir lime leaves in Asian markets. MAKES 4–6 SERVINGS

1 tablespoon coconut oil

1 tablespoon grated fresh ginger

3 garlic cloves, minced

1 small Thai chile, seeded and minced

4 cups coconut milk

1 cup chicken stock

1 teaspoon fish sauce

1 tablespoon chopped fresh Thai basil

1 tablespoon chopped fresh cilantro

1 tablespoon chopped fresh lemongrass, white part only

1 kaffir lime leaf or 1 teaspoon grated lime zest

1 pound boneless, skinless chicken breast, thinly sliced

1 teaspoon salt

Freshly ground black pepper

Juice of 1 medium lime (about 1½ tablespoons)

2 scallions, white and green parts finely sliced

1. Heat the coconut oil in a large saucepan over medium heat. Add the ginger and garlic and sauté until they become aromatic but not brown, about 1 minute.

2. Add the chile and stir well. Sauté for 1 minute.

3. Stir in the coconut milk and stock. Bring to a simmer. Add the fish sauce, basil, cilantro, lemongrass, and lime leaf. Cover and simmer for 20 minutes.

4. Pick out and discard the lime leaf. Using an immersion blender, blend the soup into a smooth purée. Alternatively, remove the solids with a slotted spoon and place them in a blender or food processor. Purée until smooth and return to the pan.

5. Bring the mixture back to a simmer and add the chicken. Cook until the chicken is firm and cooked through, about 15 minutes. Stir in the salt, pepper to taste, and lime juice. Garnish with the scallions and serve hot.

FILIPINO CHICKEN CURRY

Aficionados of Thai or Indian curries will find that this curry is only mildly hot, and unlike Thai or Vietnamese versions, it does not make use of any peanuts, peanut oil, or sour flavors. The result is a delicate curry that doesn't overwhelm the senses but is warmly comforting — great for a midwinter supper. Serve with Jasmine Rice (page 132). MAKES 4 SERVINGS

½ cup coconut oil

2 pounds boneless, skinless chicken thighs, cut into 2-inch pieces

Salt and freshly ground black pepper

1 large Yukon Gold potato, peeled and chopped into 2-inch cubes

3 celery stalks, cut into 2-inch lengths

1 small red bell pepper, seeded and cut into 2-inch pieces

1 small green bell pepper, seeded and cut into 2-inch pieces

1 medium onion, chopped

4 garlic cloves, minced

1 (1-inch) piece fresh ginger, peeled and grated

2 tablespoons Pinoy curry powder or S&B Oriental Curry Powder

1 cup chicken stock

2 tablespoons patis (Filipino fish sauce) or fish sauce

2 cups coconut milk

1. Heat ¼ cup of the coconut oil in a large deep skillet over medium heat for 1 minute .

2. Season the chicken pieces well with salt and black pepper and then add them to the skillet. Fry until lightly golden brown, 5 to 7 minutes per side, then remove from the pan and set aside.

3. Add the remaining ¼ cup coconut oil to the pan and then the potatoes. Fry until lightly golden brown on all sides, 10 to 12 minutes, then remove from the pan and set aside.

4. Add the celery to the pan and fry until it is lightly golden brown and begins to soften, about 5 minutes. Add the red and green bell peppers and fry for 5 minutes.

5. Stir in the onion and garlic and fry, stirring occasionally, until the onion softens, 4 to 5 minutes. Add the ginger and fry for 1 minute longer, then sprinkle the curry powder over this mixture and cook, stirring constantly, for 30 seconds. Add the stock and patis.

6. Return the potatoes and chicken to the pan. Bring to a simmer, then reduce the heat to medium-low and cook, covered, for 15 minutes. Add the coconut milk and simmer, uncovered, for another 15 minutes.

NOTE: *To get the best result with this chicken curry, it's important to fry the chicken and vegetables separately and add them to the pot in stages. This allows everything to brown nicely in its own time, adding both a richer hue and a deeper flavor to the finished curry.*

TRINIDAD CURRIED
CRAB AND
DUMPLINGS

Curried crab is a classic Trinidadian dish that has been adopted in other parts of the Caribbean. Traditionally, crabs are cooked whole in a water-based curry and served with large dumplings. I like to use picked crabmeat with this dish and, of course, add coconut milk to the curry sauce. Smaller potato dumplings, very much in the German style, are perfect for grabbing the sauce and making the dish heartier, without the tough texture of traditional flour dumplings. MAKES 4 SERVINGS

dumplings

2 large russet potatoes, peeled and roughly chopped

1 egg

2¼ cups all-purpose flour, or more as needed

1 tablespoon plus 1 teaspoon salt

⅛ teaspoon ground nutmeg

⅓ cup plain breadcrumbs

6 cups water

curried crab

1 tablespoon coconut oil

1 large shallot, minced

2 garlic cloves, minced

1 teaspoon finely chopped fresh thyme

½ Scotch bonnet chile, seeded and minced (optional)

2 tablespoons West Indian curry powder or madras curry powder

2 cups coconut milk

2 pounds lump crabmeat

1 teaspoon coarse salt

recipe continues on the next page

CRAB AND DUMPLINGS

continued

make the dumplings

1. Place the potatoes in a large saucepan and add enough water to cover. Bring the water to a boil, then reduce heat to a simmer and cook the potatoes for 25 to 35 minutes or until tender. Drain the potatoes and let cool.

2. When the potatoes are cooled, mash in a large bowl. Add the egg to the potatoes and beat the mixture well with a fork.

3. Whisk together the flour, 1 teaspoon of the salt, and the nutmeg in a large bowl. Add it to the potato mixture and mix well. Add the breadcrumbs and mix thoroughly. The mixture should hold together but not be overly sticky. If it is too sticky, add more flour, 1 teaspoon at a time, until it comes together and holds cleanly.

4. Wet your hands with cool water and form the potato mixture into small balls, about the size of a cherry tomato.

5. Bring the 6 cups water to a boil in a large pot and add the remaining 1 tablespoon salt. Add the dumplings and simmer until they bob to the surface, 2 to 3 minutes. Remove with a slotted spoon and set aside.

make the curried crab

6. Heat the coconut oil in a large deep pot over medium heat for 1 minute. Add the shallot and garlic and fry for 2 minutes.

7. Stir in the thyme and the chile, if using, and mix well. Stir in the curry powder and cook, stirring constantly, until the curry releases its aromas, about 30 seconds.

8. Stir in the coconut milk. Bring to a simmer and then reduce the heat to medium-low. Add the crab, dumplings, and salt. Cover the pot and simmer for 10 minutes. Serve hot in a deep soup plate.

the curry chronicles

Curry is a catchall term for a mixture of spices, either wet or dry, generally used in a stew-like preparation. I've always found a couple of things interesting about curry. First, wherever it is found worldwide, it is almost universally hot via the addition of chiles, and second, more often than not you are likely to find coconut milk as the creamy basis for curry. That is certainly true of Thai and South Indian curries, and it is a practice increasingly being adopted in other regions that may not have done so before, like the Caribbean. Whether a native convention or an adopted one, it is certainly true that the slightly sweet flavor and rich consistency of coconut milk tempers the extremely bold flavors of curry.

THAI-KAENG PHET GAI
(PUMPKIN RED CURRY WITH CHICKEN)

Pumpkin red curry is my favorite Thai curry bar none. The key to this flavorful dish is not to skimp on the coconut milk, which acts as a mild base to the spicy curry. While you can certainly substitute butternut squash or (preferably) Cinderella pumpkin for the kabocha squash, try to get the kabocha — its unique, almost russet potato–like consistency and deep sweetness make the dish. Serve with Jasmine Rice (page 132).

MAKES 4 SERVINGS

1 (14-ounce) can coconut cream

2 tablespoons red curry paste

3 kaffir lime leaves or 1 tablespoon grated lime zest

1 teaspoon coconut sugar

1 teaspoon fish sauce

1 (14-ounce) can coconut milk

1 (1-pound) kabocha squash, peeled, seeded, and cut into pieces ¼ inch thick and 2 inches wide

2 pounds boneless, skinless chicken breast, thinly sliced

1 cup green beans, trimmed and cut in half crosswise

1 cup loosely packed fresh Thai basil (or regular basil in a pinch)

1. Pour the coconut cream into a large deep pot over medium heat. When it melts and begins to bubble and simmer, add the red curry paste. Mix well and cook until the paste begins to break down, 3 to 4 minutes.

2. Stir in the lime leaves, coconut sugar, fish sauce, and coconut milk, and mix well. Simmer for 2 to 3 minutes.

3. Add the squash and chicken. Reduce the heat to medium-low and simmer, uncovered, for 15 minutes. Stir in the green beans and basil and cook until the chicken is cooked through and the squash is tender, about 10 minutes longer.

VIETNAMESE CHICKEN AND YAM CURRY

I've seen this curry made with taro, regular potatoes, and orange sweet potatoes, but I like to make it with Asian sweet potatoes, called Murasaki potatoes, which have a more solid texture and a subtly sweet taste. This recipe uses Vietnamese curry, which is sold in Asian grocery stores under the name *ca ri ni an do*. If you can't find it, substitute madras curry powder instead. Though you can serve this with rice, Vietnamese curries tend to be served with crusty baguette-like bread.

MAKES 4 SERVINGS

2 tablespoons grated fresh ginger

2 teaspoons coarse salt

2 teaspoons sugar

½ teaspoon red pepper flakes

3 tablespoons Vietnamese curry powder

1 large onion, finely chopped

4 garlic cloves, minced

2 pounds skinless bone-in chicken thighs

¼ cup safflower oil or vegetable oil, or more as needed

1½ pounds Asian sweet potatoes, peeled and cut into 1-inch chunks

2 large carrots, peeled and cut into 1-inch chunks

1 cup chicken broth

1 teaspoon fish sauce

2 stalks fresh lemongrass

4 kaffir lime leaves or 1½ teaspoons grated lime zest

2 cups coconut milk

¼ cup chopped fresh cilantro for garnish

1. Mix together the ginger, salt, sugar, red pepper flakes, 1 table-spoon of the curry powder, half of the onion, and half of the garlic in a large bowl. Add the chicken and mix well to coat. Cover with plastic wrap and refrigerate for at least 6 hours or up to overnight.

2. Heat the oil in a large deep saucepan over medium heat. Add the sweet potato and carrots and fry until they are lightly brown on all sides, 4 to 5 minutes. Do not layer the vegetables in the pan; cook in batches, if needed. Remove the sweet potatoes and carrots and set aside.

3. Add the chicken to the pan and brown the pieces on both sides, 6 to 7 minutes per side. Remove from the pan and set aside.

4. Slice the lemongrass stalks in half lengthwise and gently pound with the back of a heavy knife. Add a little more oil to the pan, if needed, then add the remaining onion and garlic. Sauté until the onion begins to soften, 1 to 2 minutes. Add the remaining 2 tablespoons curry powder, stir well, and fry for 30 seconds. Add the broth, fish sauce, lemongrass, and lime leaves. Return the chicken, potatoes, and carrots to the pan. Bring to a simmer, cover, and cook until the chicken is tender, 20 to 30 minutes.

5. Add the coconut milk to the pan and mix well. Simmer 5 minutes longer. Serve in a large deep bowl garnished with the cilantro.

GLUTEN-FREE

DAIRY-FREE

GOAN
FISH CURRY

The coconut sauce that is the basis of this spicy curry comes not from premade coconut milk but from a quick sauce made with seasoned toasted coconut. The dish is traditionally made with pomfret, a plentiful butterfish found in the Indian Ocean. You can substitute another variety of butterfish if you can get it, but any firm-fleshed white fish — like tilapia or red snapper — will work well, too. Serve with Persian-Style Basmati Rice (page 131) and Coconut Chutney (page 106). MAKES 4 SERVINGS

2 tablespoons coriander seeds

2 teaspoons cumin seeds

2 small dried red chiles, stemmed

½ cup grated fresh coconut

3 tablespoons grated fresh ginger

3 tablespoons grated garlic

1 tablespoon tamarind pulp concentrate

1 tablespoon sugar

2 cups water, or more as needed

1½ pounds boneless pomfret or tilapia

2 tablespoons coconut oil

1 small onion, thinly sliced

1 small green chile, seeded and minced

1 teaspoon coarse salt

1 tablespoon malt vinegar

1. Heat a medium skillet over medium heat. Add the coriander seeds, cumin seeds, and whole red chiles. Toast by swirling the spices in the pan until they begin to release their aromas, 30 seconds to 1 minute. Remove from the heat and let cool.

2. Place the cooled spices in a food processor or high-powered blender. Add the coconut, ginger, garlic, tamarind pulp concentrate, sugar, and ½ cup of the water. Grind the mixture into a thick paste, adding more water as necessary to achieve the consistency of thick batter (you will still see flecks of coconut in the paste).

3. Divide the seasoning paste into two portions and smear half on the fish. Cover the fish with plastic wrap and set aside.

4. Heat the coconut oil in a large deep skillet over medium-low heat. Add the onion and fry, stirring as needed, until the onion is deeply golden brown, 7 to 8 minutes. Add the green chile, mix well, and fry for 30 seconds.

5. Add the remaining seasoning paste to the pan and mix well. Sauté the paste, stirring often, until it begins to release a rich aroma, 3 to 5 minutes. Stir in the remaining 1½ cups water.

6. Add the fish and bring to a simmer. Cook gently until the fish is cooked through and firm, 15 to 20 minutes. Stir in the salt and vinegar.

the cuisine of goa

Goa, in southern India, is known for its prodigious use of coconut milk and coconut products in its spicy cuisine. The cuisine is also highly influenced by the foodways of the region's former Portuguese colonial rulers. If you find this dish is too spicy (Goan cuisine is known for its heat), reduce the amount of chiles to your liking.

COCONUT
CHUTNEY

GLUTEN-FREE

DAIRY-FREE

PALEO-FRIENDLY

This classic South Indian recipe is a favorite condiment for all kinds of foods, from the large lentil or rice flour crêpes called *dosas* to curries and rice dishes. It is a lovely, cooling side sauce for barbecue or even a delicious dipping sauce for flatbreads or pita chips. Caramelize the shallot very well, as it adds extra sweetness to the chutney without adding any sugar.   MAKES ABOUT 2 CUPS

1   cup grated fresh or frozen coconut

½   cup water

2   tablespoons coconut oil

1   small shallot, finely sliced

1   garlic clove, finely chopped

⅓   teaspoon mustard seeds

½   teaspoon finely minced green chile

5   fresh curry leaves

1. Combine the coconut and water in a food processor or blender and blend until you achieve a creamy consistency. You will still see plenty of coconut particles. Pour into a deep bowl and set aside.

2. Heat the coconut oil in a small skillet over medium heat. Add the shallot and decrease the heat to medium-low. Cook slowly until the shallot is deep brown and caramelized, 4 to 5 minutes. Add the garlic, stir well, and cook for 1 minute longer.

3. Add the mustard seeds, chile, and curry leaves. Fry just until the mustard seeds begin to pop, about 2 minutes. Remove the pan from the heat.

4. Pour the shallot mixture into the bowl of puréed coconut and mix well. Allow to cool completely and serve. Unused chutney can be stored in an airtight container in the refrigerator for up to 2 weeks, or in the freezer for 1 month.

SRI LANKAN
MEATBALL CURRY

This extremely popular curry melds Sri Lanka's South Asian roots and the meatballs brought to the island by Dutch colonists. The pleasantly spicy sauce is complex in flavor thanks to the addition of whole cardamom and cinnamon spices and both curry leaves and fenugreek leaves, which can be found in Asian grocery stores. Try not to omit these, as they are the underpinnings of the curry's flavor. Serve with rice.

MAKES 4 SERVINGS

meatballs

- 2 pounds ground turkey or chicken
- 1 shallot, grated
- 1 tablespoon grated fresh ginger
- 4 garlic cloves, minced
- 2 teaspoons ground turmeric
- 1 teaspoon paprika
- 1 teaspoon freshly ground black pepper
- 1 egg
- ⅓ cup plain breadcrumbs, or more as needed
- ¼ cup coconut oil for frying

curry sauce

- 1 large onion, minced
- 2 garlic cloves, minced
- 2 tablespoons grated fresh ginger
- 2 green cardamom pods, mashed
- 1 (2-inch) cinnamon stick
- 2 tablespoons madras curry powder
- 1 teaspoon cayenne pepper
- 2 teaspoons ground turmeric
- ½ cup crushed tomatoes
- ½ cup water
- 2 cups coconut milk
- 8 fresh curry leaves
- 1 tablespoon dried fenugreek leaves

  Salt

1. To make the meatballs, combine the turkey, shallot, ginger, garlic, turmeric, paprika, and black pepper in a large bowl. Add the egg and mix well, then add enough breadcrumbs for the mixture to hold together when formed into a ball. Knead well. Form into meatballs about the size of golf balls and set aside.

2. Heat the coconut oil in a large deep pot over medium-low heat. Place the meatballs gently in the pan and fry until deeply browned, 4 to 5 minutes per side. Gently remove the browned meatballs with a slotted spoon and place on a plate lined with paper towels.

3. To make the curry sauce, add the onion, garlic, and ginger to the same pot in which you made the meatballs. Fry until the onions begin to soften, 2 to 3 minutes.

4. Add the cardamom, cinnamon stick, curry powder, cayenne, and turmeric, and fry for 1 minute, stirring often.

5. Mix in the crushed tomatoes and water and stir well. Add the meatballs and simmer for 15 minutes.

6. Stir in the coconut milk, curry leaves, and fenugreek leaves. Season with salt to taste and simmer for 2 to 3 minutes longer. Serve hot.

4
vegetables, legumes, and starches

I often think about the fact that the flesh of the coconut is called the "meat," given that coconut is such a good substitute for meat in many dishes. Its richness, texture, and satisfying taste make it an excellent substitute for animal products, and an ideal ingredient in a vegan or vegetarian kitchen. But even for those who are omnivores or who are simply seeking interesting side dishes, the addition of coconut can elevate common vegetables and starches to new heights and make them stars of the plate. In this section, you'll find recipes for everyday vegetables, sides, and legumes as well as some that might be a bit more exotic, in which case I usually give a substitution. In addition to coconut-based side dishes, I've included some basic recipes for side dishes that complement other recipes in this book, such as plain basmati and jasmine rice.

ASPARAGUS
WITH SHALLOTS AND SHREDDED COCONUT

GLUTEN-FREE

DAIRY-FREE

PALEO-FRIENDLY

Most recipes use whole asparagus, but the asparagus in this dish has been cut into bite-size pieces so that it melds better with the other ingredients. This is a delightful side dish for fish or chicken, or as part of a vegan spread. It also can be eaten as the primary dish, perhaps with basmati rice or even with pita or naan as an Indian-style vegetarian main course. MAKES 4 SERVINGS

1 tablespoon coconut oil

1 large shallot, minced

1 bunch asparagus, chopped into 1-inch pieces

1 small red chile, minced

½ teaspoon mustard seeds

¼ cup dried unsweetened shredded coconut

1 teaspoon madras curry powder

1 cup water

1. Heat the coconut oil in a large skillet over medium-low heat. Add the shallot and asparagus and fry until the asparagus starts to lightly brown, 4 to 5 minutes.

2. Add the chile and mustard seeds and fry until the mustard seeds start to pop, about 3 minutes.

3. Stir in the coconut and mix well. Cook, stirring constantly, for 2 to 3 minutes. Mix in the madras curry powder and fry for 1 minute longer.

4. Pour the water into the pan and reduce the heat to low. Simmer until all the water is absorbed, 10 to 12 minutes. Serve hot.

ZUCCHINI
WITH MUSTARD SEED, GRATED COCONUT, AND TURMERIC

Marrying the South Asian flavors of tamarind, coconut, and mustard seeds creates a tart, creamy, pungent side dish or vegetarian/vegan main dish. I recommend using my favorite type of zucchini, the Lebanese kusa variety, sometimes called "gray zucchini." The flesh of kusa is a bit firmer and the taste sweeter and more distinct than that of regular varieties. It is easily found in Latino and Middle Eastern markets and is recognizable by its pale pistachio-colored skin and fatter, squatter body. MAKES 4 SERVINGS

2 teaspoons coconut oil

1 small red onion, finely chopped

2 garlic cloves, thinly sliced

4 fresh curry leaves

4 large Lebanese kusa or 2 large traditional green zucchini, cut into 1-inch chunks

½ teaspoon coarse salt

½ teaspoon freshly ground black pepper

1 teaspoon mustard seeds

1 teaspoon ground turmeric

½ cup grated fresh or frozen coconut

¼ cup vegetable broth

¼ cup water

2 teaspoons tamarind syrup

1 tablespoon sugar

Roughly chopped fresh cilantro for garnish (optional)

1. Heat a large skillet over high heat and add the coconut oil. Reduce the heat to medium and add the onion. Fry until the onion just begins to soften, 2 minutes. Add the garlic and fry for 1 minute. Add the curry leaves and fry for 30 seconds.

2. Stir in the zucchini and mix until all of the pieces are coated in oil, then season with the salt and pepper. Cook the zucchini until it is just beginning to brown, 4 to 5 minutes. Add the mustard seeds and cook until the seeds begin to pop, 1 to 2 minutes. Mix in the turmeric. This will make the mixture very dry. Cook until the turmeric begins to release its aromas, about 30 seconds.

3. Stir in the coconut and broth. Reduce the heat to low and cook, uncovered, until roughly half of the liquid is absorbed, about 15 minutes.

4. While the vegetables are cooking, combine the water, tamarind syrup, and sugar in a small saucepan over medium heat. Simmer until thickened and reduced by half, 10 to 12 minutes. You should have a thin syrup.

5. Remove the zucchini from the heat and spoon into a large flat dish. Drizzle with the tamarind sauce. Garnish with the chopped cilantro, if using, and serve.

ROASTED CAULIFLOWER
WITH COCONUT AND GREEN CHILES

GLUTEN-FREE

DAIRY-FREE

PALEO-FRIENDLY

In my opinion, cauliflower is entirely undersung as a versatile vegetable. It lends itself well to being fried, stewed, curried, baked, roasted, and puréed. In this recipe, I use warm spices as the flavoring for richly caramelized cauliflower that is then tossed with crisped green chiles, garlic, and toasted coconut. I find that it's hearty enough to be an entrée. MAKES 4–6 SERVINGS

2 cups white cauliflower florets

2 cups orange cauliflower florets

2 cups purple cauliflower florets

¼ cup extra-virgin olive oil

1 teaspoon ground coriander

1 teaspoon ground cumin

1 teaspoon ground turmeric

Salt and freshly ground black pepper

1 tablespoon coconut oil

4 garlic cloves, thinly sliced

2 small green chiles, thinly sliced

½ cup toasted unsweetened coconut flakes

1. Preheat the oven to 400°F (200°C).

2. Place the cauliflower florets in a large baking dish or on a sheet pan with high sides and drizzle them with the olive oil. Season with the coriander, cumin, and turmeric. Add salt and pepper to taste and mix well.

3. Roast the cauliflower in the oven until it is deeply golden brown, 20 to 30 minutes.

4. While the cauliflower is roasting, heat the coconut oil in a small skillet over medium heat. Add the garlic and chile and fry until the garlic is golden brown, 1 to 2 minutes.

5. Arrange the cauliflower on a platter and toss with the fried garlic and chile and the toasted coconut.

KABOCHA SQUASH PURÉE

WITH COCONUT AND KOREAN CHILE

I got the idea for this purée from a common Trinidadian pumpkin dish usually served for breakfast with roti, a flatbread. In that iteration, the pumpkin is cooked down with onions, garlic, and spices until it becomes a mash. My version uses kabocha squash, a favorite of mine for its delicately sweet flavor and almost fluffy texture, and *gochujang*, a fermented chile paste made in Korea. Try serving this purée as a unique side dish at Thanksgiving. MAKES 4–6 SERVINGS

2 tablespoons coconut oil

1 small kabocha squash, peeled, seeded, and chopped into large chunks

1 shallot, minced

2 garlic cloves, minced

1 teaspoon finely chopped fresh thyme

¼ cup chicken stock or vegetable stock

1 teaspoon gochujang paste

⅓ cup coconut milk

Salt

1. Heat a large deep saucepan over medium-low heat. Add the coconut oil and heat for 30 seconds, then add the squash. Sauté for 10 minutes. Stir in the shallot, garlic, and thyme and mix well.

2. Add the stock and reduce the heat to low. Cover the pan and simmer the squash until it is fork-tender, 20 to 25 minutes.

3. Place the squash pieces in a food processor and process to a smooth paste. Return the purée to the pan and whisk in the gochujang, coconut milk, and salt to taste. Bring to a simmer over medium-low heat and cook gently for 3 to 5 minutes. Serve hot.

TEMPURA CAULIFLOWER
WITH COCONUT HARISSA SAUCE

Here is another cauliflower recipe, but this one features a crisp tempura batter to go with a spicy dipping sauce. I love using three different types of cauliflower, but this batter works equally well with any vegetable that is suitable for tempura, such as zucchini, kabocha squash, green beans, eggplant, mushrooms, and green peppers. Be sure to make the dipping sauce before you fry the cauliflower, because you'll want to eat the tempura while it's hot. MAKES 4 SERVINGS

dipping sauce

- 1 teaspoon toasted sesame oil
- ½ shallot, minced
- 1 tablespoon grated fresh ginger
- ¼ cup rice wine or sake
- ¾ cup coconut nectar
- ½ teaspoon harissa

tempura

- 1½ cups cornstarch
- 1½ cups all-purpose flour
- ½ teaspoon salt
- 1 teaspoon shichimi togarashi (see note)
- 2 egg whites
- 1 cup club soda, or more as needed
- 3 cups safflower oil or canola oil
- 3 cups cauliflower florets (no larger than 2-inch pieces)

NOTE: Shichimi togarashi *is a common Japanese seven-spice powder blend that includes chile pepper, seaweed, ginger, and orange. You can find it in Asian grocery stores.*

1. To make the dipping sauce, heat the sesame oil in a medium saucepan over medium-low heat. Add the shallot and ginger and fry for 1 minute. Stir in the rice wine and cook until the mixture is reduced by half, 2 to 4 minutes. Mix in the coconut nectar and harissa. Simmer for 2 minutes longer, stirring well. Remove from the heat and set aside.

2. To make the tempura batter, whisk together the cornstarch, flour, salt, and shichimi togarashi in a large bowl. Gently stir in the egg whites and enough club soda to bring the batter to about the consistency of pancake batter.

3. Heat the safflower oil in a deep saucepan over medium-low heat. When a drop of batter placed in the oil vigorously bubbles and rises to the surface, the oil is ready. Set a wire rack over a sheet pan or line a tray with paper towels.

4. Dip the cauliflower into the batter and coat evenly. Do not shake off the excess.

5. Drop the coated cauliflower pieces into the oil and fry until they are golden brown, 3 to 4 minutes. Remove from the oil with a slotted spoon and place on the wire rack or the tray lined with paper towels to drain. Serve hot with the dipping sauce.

TRICOLOR CARROTS
ROASTED WITH COCONUT-ORANGE GLAZE

Deeply red, yellow, and even purple heirloom carrots are as delicious as they are attractive. I love to slow-roast these carrots to bring out their sweetness and then toss them in a sweet-sour-hot glaze. This is a richly hued, addictively tasty dish for any fall supper, and for the Thanksgiving table in particular. MAKES 4 SERVINGS

2 pounds mixed yellow, orange, red, and purple carrots, scrubbed (see note)

¼ cup coconut oil, melted

1¼ tablespoons finely chopped fresh thyme

1 tablespoon coarse salt

Freshly ground or cracked black pepper

2 tablespoons unsalted butter

¾ cup coconut nectar

¼ cup Seville orange juice or equal parts orange, grapefruit, and lime juices to equal ¼ cup

½ teaspoon red pepper flakes

2 tablespoons grated orange zest

¼ cup fresh parsley

1. Preheat the oven to 325°F (165°C).

2. Slice the carrots, on a bias, into 1-inch pieces and place in a large bowl. Toss with the coconut oil, thyme, salt, and black pepper to taste. Mix well so that all the carrots are well coated. Spread on a sheet pan or baking dish in one layer.

3. Roast the carrots in the oven until they are browned and tender, 20 to 30 minutes.

4. While the carrots are roasting, melt the butter in a medium saucepan over medium heat and add the coconut nectar, orange juice, and red pepper flakes. Simmer until the liquid is reduced by one-quarter and thickened, 6 to 7 minutes.

5. Remove the carrots from the oven and pour the sauce over the carrots. Return the carrots to the oven and roast for 5 to 10 minutes longer, or until most of the glaze is absorbed. Remove from the oven and mix in the orange zest.

6. Arrange the carrots on a platter and garnish evenly with the parsley.

NOTE: *You'll notice I scrub my carrots rather than peel them; this is because the outer skin is full of nutrients. Of course, you can peel yours if you like.*

DAL MAKHANI
(BLACK LENTILS IN COCONUT-TOMATO-MASALA SAUCE)

This dish is the vegan counterpart to Coconut Tikka Masala (page 80) and tastes so good you won't miss the meat. Black lentils (also called *urad dal*) have a toothsome, nutty flavor that makes for a hearty dish. Asafetida is a powdered herb that is usually added to beans in Indian cooking. It imparts a subtle flavor, but more importantly, it reduces gastric disturbances that eating a lot of beans might sometimes cause. Serve with white basmati rice or naan bread. MAKES 4 SERVINGS

5 cups water

1½ cups black lentils (urad dal), picked over to remove any small stones, then rinsed and drained

1 bay leaf

¼ teaspoon asafetida (optional)

1 tablespoon coconut oil

1½ teaspoons minced garlic

1½ teaspoons minced fresh ginger

1 tablespoon tomato paste

1 tablespoon garam masala

1 cup coconut milk

1 cup coconut cream

1 teaspoon salt

1 tablespoon dried fenugreek leaves

1. Bring the water to a boil in a large saucepan over high heat. Add the lentils, then reduce the heat to a simmer. Add the bay leaf and the asafetida, if using. Cook the lentils until tender, about 30 minutes, skimming off any white froth that forms on the surface.

2. Drain the lentils and rinse with cool water. Discard the bay leaf.

3. To make the sauce, heat a medium saucepan over high heat. Add the coconut oil, garlic, and ginger, and fry for 30 seconds. Add the tomato paste and cook, stirring, for 1 minute. Add the garam masala and cook, stirring, for 30 seconds.

4. Slowly drizzle the coconut milk and coconut cream into the tomato paste mixture, whisking constantly until the mixture is completely smooth. Add the salt and the cooked lentils. When the mixture reaches a simmer, reduce the heat to low and simmer gently for 10 minutes.

5. Rub the fenugreek leaves together between your palms and add to the saucepan. Simmer for 1 minute.

COCONUT
BOSTON BAKED BEANS

GLUTEN-FREE

DAIRY-FREE

Boston baked beans are a quintessentially comforting American dish that brings to mind low and slow hearth cooking. Molasses is the traditional flavoring for baked beans, but my version uses coconut nectar instead. The result is a somewhat lighter version of the classic dish. Serve these beans with some good, crusty white bread or cornbread for a more total meal.

MAKES 4 SERVINGS

- 2 cups dried or canned navy beans (if using dried, soak in 6 cups water overnight)
- ½ pound slab bacon or turkey bacon, diced
- 1 medium onion, diced
- 2 garlic cloves, minced
- 2 teaspoons tomato paste
- 2 teaspoons dry mustard
- 1 teaspoon freshly ground black pepper
- 2 tablespoons brown sugar
- ½ cup coconut nectar
- 3 sprigs fresh thyme
- Boiling water (5 cups for dried beans or 3 cups for canned beans)
- Salt

1. Preheat the oven to 275°F (135°C). If using presoaked dried beans, parboil them: Bring 6 cups of water to a boil in a large pot. Drain the soaked beans and add them to the boiling water, then reduce the heat to a simmer. Cook the beans until they are just tender, about 30 minutes. Drain and set aside.

2. Heat a large ovenproof pot, like a Dutch oven, over medium-low heat. Add the bacon and fry until it is nicely brown and the fat is rendered, 5 to 6 minutes.

3. Add the onion and garlic and fry until the onion begins to soften, 1 to 2 minutes. Stir in the tomato paste and fry for 1 minute. Stir in the mustard, pepper, and brown sugar, and fry for 1 minute longer.

4. Add the beans, coconut nectar, thyme, and boiling water. Stir well. Cover the pot, place it in the oven, and bake until the beans are very tender (4 hours if using dried beans and 2½ hours if using canned).

5. Remove the pot from the oven and stir in salt to taste. Return the pot to the oven and bake, uncovered, for another 30 to 40 minutes.

TOASTED CHICKPEAS
WITH MIXED GREENS IN COCONUT SAUCE

I came up with this recipe one summer when my garden produced an overabundance of greens. Out of options, I decided to experiment with cooking them in the same method that is used for *callaloo*, a West African stew made from chopped taro leaves and coconut milk. You can use any type of greens you like, but I think the slightly bitter bite of collards or mustard greens really complements the caramelized sweetness of the onion and garlic. Serve hot as a side dish or as a main dish with crusty bread. MAKES 4 SERVINGS

2 tablespoons coconut oil

1 (15-ounce) can chickpeas, rinsed and drained, or ⅓ cup dried chickpeas, soaked and simmered (see note)

½ teaspoon ground cumin

1 small onion, thinly sliced

2 garlic cloves, thinly sliced

6 cups mixed greens, such as collards, mustard, kale, or chard, roughly chopped

1 teaspoon coarse salt
   Freshly ground black pepper

¼ cup water

1 cup coconut milk

1. Heat the coconut oil in a large skillet over medium-low heat. Stir in the chickpeas and fry gently until they are lightly browned on all sides, 4 to 5 minutes. Stir in the cumin and fry for 30 seconds. Add the onion and garlic and fry until the onions begin to soften, 3 to 4 minutes.

2. Stir in the mixed greens, salt, and pepper to taste. Reduce the heat to low and add the water. Cover and allow the greens to braise until they soften, about 20 minutes.

3. Add the coconut milk and mix well. Increase the heat to medium-low and simmer, uncovered, until the coconut milk is reduced by half, about 10 minutes.

NOTE: *If you're using dried chickpeas — which I think have a better flavor — you'll want to soak them in 1 cup of water overnight. The next day, bring 1 cup of water to a boil, drain the beans, and add them to the boiling water. Simmer the beans until they are tender, about 1 hour. You can add a pinch of baking soda to the cooking water to soften up the beans more quickly. I often prepare dried beans and then drain and freeze them in ziplock bags so I have them ready whenever I want them. To use, I simply defrost them by dropping the frozen beans into some boiling water for 1 minute.*

BREADFRUIT
OIL DOWN

Oil down is a traditional method of simmering starchy vegetables and fruits with a piece of salted meat in coconut milk until the milk is totally absorbed and only the oil of the milk is left at the bottom of the pot. If you can't find fresh breadfruit, look for it canned or frozen in Caribbean and Indian markets; you can also substitute yucca. *Aji dulce*, or "seasoning pepper," is found in Caribbean and Latino markets as well. This dish is hearty enough for an excellent winter or fall supper. MAKES 4 SERVINGS

1 tablespoon coconut oil

2 shallots, minced

2 ají dulce peppers, seeded and minced

2 garlic cloves, minced

¼ pound smoked ham or smoked turkey, cut into cubes

2 cups chopped dasheen (taro) leaves or collard greens (optional)

½ pound lean boneless pork round or turkey breast, cut into ½-inch pieces

4 fresh culantro or cilantro leaves

1 teaspoon fresh thyme

4 cups coconut milk

1 large breadfruit, peeled and chopped into large chunks, or 20 ounces canned or frozen breadfruit pieces, drained, or 2 large yucca, peeled and cut into large chunks

2 teaspoons salt

1. Heat the coconut oil in a large pot over medium heat. Add the shallots, peppers, garlic, and ham, and sauté until the shallots begin to soften, 1 to 2 minutes.

2. Add the dasheen leaves, if using, and reduce the heat to medium-low. Stir well and cook, covered, until the dasheen begins to reduce and soften, about 5 minutes.

3. Stir in the pork, culantro, thyme, and coconut milk and mix well. Bring to a simmer. Add the breadfruit, cover, and simmer until the breadfruit has totally absorbed the coconut milk and only a little oil is left in the pan, 30 to 40 minutes. Stir in the salt and serve hot.

caribbean staples

Breadfruit, jackfruit, and yucca (cassava) were the staples of nutrition for the enslaved, and later indentured, workforce of the Caribbean. These starchy fruits were cheap and plentiful, and they filled the belly with carbohydrates that kept workers going for long and brutal hours. This history, coupled with the diverse cultural heritage in the Caribbean (Spanish, French, West African, East Indian, Chinese, and native Caribbean), means that there are more recipes for these ingredients than you can count. Often, coconut products — also plentiful, with the advantage of being nutritionally dense — rounded out the preparations.

VEGETABLE
KORMA

GLUTEN-FREE

DAIRY-FREE

PALEO-FRIENDLY

This variation on chicken korma puts seasonal vegetables to good use. Meatier vegetables like eggplant and squash are ideal, but root vegetables like carrot and potato are equally good. The best vegetable kormas feature a variety of vegetables, and I've made this dish with a mix of cauliflower, zucchini, and even green beans. Experiment to find which combinations you like best. Serve with Persian-Style Basmati Rice (page 131). MAKES 4 SERVINGS

2 tablespoons coconut oil

1 small onion, thinly sliced

2 garlic cloves, minced

1 tablespoon grated fresh ginger

3 green cardamom pods, crushed slightly

1 small dried chile

1 tablespoon garam masala

1 teaspoon ground turmeric

1 medium eggplant, peeled and cut into large cubes

½ pound green beans, cut into 1-inch pieces

1 medium potato, peeled and cut into 1-inch cubes

1 teaspoon salt

1½ cups water

3 tablespoons almond butter

1 large yellow squash, cut into large cubes

1½ cups coconut milk

1. Heat the coconut oil in a large saucepan over medium heat. Add the onion and fry until it begins to soften, 2 to 3 minutes.

2. Add the garlic and ginger and fry, stirring constantly, until just fragrant, about 1 minute. Stir in the cardamom, chile, garam masala, and tumeric, and fry for 1 minute longer, stirring constantly.

3. Add the eggplant, green beans, and potato to the pan and mix well. Fry until the pieces begin to brown on all sides, 3 to 4 minutes. Stir in the salt and mix well.

4. Stir in the water. Bring to a simmer and cook until the water reduces by half, 10 to 12 minutes.

5. Stir in the almond butter and mix well. Simmer for 2 minutes so that the almond butter breaks up and you have smooth, thick sauce.

6. Add the squash and the coconut milk and mix thoroughly. Simmer for 10 minutes longer. The sauce should be thick and creamy and pale yellow or beige in color.

COCONUT
POTATO
CURRY

This potato curry is slightly tangy thanks to the crushed tomato and tomato paste. Fenugreek, an herb that is integral to a lot of Indian cooking, really makes this dish. You can find it fresh or dried in Indian markets. If you can't find fenugreek, use cilantro. This is a good side dish, or serve it with naan or pita bread as an entrée. MAKES 4 SERVINGS

2 tablespoons coconut oil

4 medium Yukon Gold or sweet potatoes, scrubbed and cut into chunks

1 small yellow onion, minced

2 garlic cloves, minced

1 tablespoon grated fresh ginger

1 teaspoon ground coriander

1 teaspoon ground cumin

½ teaspoon ground turmeric

1 small green chile, minced

2 teaspoons tomato paste

1 cup crushed tomatoes

1½ cups water, vegetable stock, or chicken stock

1 cup coconut milk

1 teaspoon coarse salt

1 tablespoon finely chopped fresh fenugreek or 1 teaspoon dried, or 1 tablespoon finely chopped fresh cilantro

1. Heat the coconut oil in a large skillet over medium heat and add the potatoes. Fry until lightly browned on all sides, 6 to 7 minutes.

2. Stir in the onion and fry for 1 to 2 minutes. Add the garlic and ginger and fry for 1 minute.

3. Stir in the coriander, cumin, turmeric, and chile, and mix well. Cook for 1 minute.

4. Stir in the tomato paste and cook for 2 minutes, stirring often.

5. Add the crushed tomatoes and water. Bring to a simmer, then reduce the heat and cook, uncovered, until the potatoes are fork-tender and most of the liquid is absorbed, 20 to 25 minutes.

6. Add the coconut milk and salt and stir well. Rub the fenugreek between your palms, then stir it into the mixture. Simmer for 10 minutes.

PERSIAN-STYLE
BASMATI RICE

GLUTEN-FREE

DAIRY-FREE

Persians are known for perfect rice in which every grain is separate, long, dry, and fluffy. The secret is a steaming method that traps the excess moisture away from the rice as it cooks. While the oil may seem excessive, it's absolutely necessary to get the prized *tahdig* crust at the bottom of the rice. When you remove the tahdig, enjoy it plain, or drizzle a little sauce from your main dish on top for a delicious appetizer. MAKES 6–8 SERVINGS

2 cups high-quality basmati rice, such as Lal Qilla brand

6½ cups water

1 tablespoon coarse salt

¼ cup plus 2 tablespoons coconut oil

VARIATION:
INDIAN-SPICED RICE

When I'm making Indian dishes, I add a cinnamon stick and two cardamom pods to the rice as it boils. I then lightly sauté golden raisins, fresh peas, and slivered almonds (about ¼ cup of each) in 1 tablespoon of butter. I mix these in with the rice before I "mound" it for steaming.

1. To wash the rice, place it in a deep bowl and add enough cold water to cover by 3 inches. Swirl the rice around with your hand until the water is cloudy. Carefully drain the water. Repeat this four or five times, until the water runs clear. Set the rice aside.

2. Bring 6 cups of the water to a boil in a large nonstick saucepan or a large iron pot. Add the salt, 1 tablespoon of the oil, and the rice, and simmer over medium-low heat for 10 to 15 minutes. Drain in a fine-mesh seive.

3. Add ¼ cup of the water and 1 tablespoon of the oil to the rice pot. Swirl it around. Place a large spoonful of rice in the middle of the pot and continue adding spoonfuls in a mound until all the rice is used. Drizzle the remaining ¼ cup oil over the rice and pour the remaining ¼ cup water over it. Use a rubber spatula to smooth the mound into a pyramid.

4. Place a clean dish towel or doubled-up paper towels over the pot and squeeze the lid into place. Do not allow the cloth to droop over the sides; instead, fold it up over the top of the lid like a bundle. Cook the rice over low heat until the rice grains appear fat and fluffy, 25 to 30 minutes.

5. Spoon the rice onto a platter. To remove the tahdig (rice crust) on the bottom of the pan, place the bottom of the pot under cold water, then use a spatula to carefully loosen the crust. Turn it out onto a platter and serve.

JASMINE
RICE

Jasmine rice is a standard accompaniment to Thai and Vietnamese foods. Longer than American rice varieties, this fragrant grain is closer in taste and texture to Indian basmati rice, although somewhat stickier. It's necessary to wash the rice thoroughly — at least four or five times — before cooking to prevent it from becoming hopelessly gloppy. I like to add a kaffir lime leaf for an extra layer of aroma and delicate taste. MAKES 8 SERVINGS

2 cups high-quality jasmine rice

3 cups water

1 tablespoon coarse salt

1 tablespoon coconut oil

1 kaffir lime leaf or 1 teaspoon grated lime zest (optional)

1. To wash the rice, place it in a deep bowl and add enough cold water to cover by 3 inches. Swirl the rice around with your hand until the water is cloudy. Carefully drain the water. Repeat this four or five times, until the water runs clear. Set the rice aside.

2. Bring the water to a boil in a large nonstick saucepan or a large iron pot. Add the salt, coconut oil, lime leaf, and rice, and simmer over medium-low heat for 10 to 15 minutes, covered, mixing once or twice. Skim off any thick white liquid that rises to the top of the rice.

3. When all of the water is absorbed, place a clean dish towel or doubled-up paper towels over the pot and then squeeze the lid into place. Do not allow the cloth to droop over the sides; instead, fold it up over the top of the lid like a bundle. Cover and cook the rice over low heat for 10 to 15 minutes longer. Remove the lid and fluff.

how to achieve fluffy rice

In this recipe, I defer to the Persian and North Indian method of steaming the rice over low heat after it has been parboiled. A cloth or layer of paper towels placed between the lid and the top of the pan captures any moisture up and away from the rice grains. It is a foolproof method for making fluffy, rather than sticky, rice.

Jasmine rice, which is used primarily in Thailand, is one of the stickier rice grains, so it's also important to wash it well before cooking to ensure a fluffy end result.

COCONUT BLACK RICE
WITH TOASTED SHALLOTS AND GARLIC

Black rice, also called "forbidden rice," is a Chinese variety that is dark black when raw but cooks up purple. The hue is an indication of anthocyanin, a powerful antioxidant found in many richly colored fruits and vegetables like eggplant, cherries, currants, acai, and some varieties of grape. The nutty-flavored firm grain also has vitamin E and iron, which makes it a nutritional powerhouse.   MAKES 4 SERVINGS

3½ cups water

1 tablespoon salt

1½ cups black rice

1 star anise pod

1 cup coconut milk

Freshly ground black pepper

1 tablespoon coconut oil

2 large shallots, thinly sliced

10 garlic cloves, thinly sliced

1 tablespoon fresh cilantro for garnish

1. Bring the water and the salt to a boil. Add the black rice, along with the star anise, and reduce the heat to medium-low. Cover and simmer the rice, occasionally skimming off any foam, until it is cooked through and tender, 45 minutes.

2. Drain the rice in a fine-mesh sieve and return it to the pot. Add the coconut milk and season with pepper. Heat over medium-low heat, uncovered and stirring often, until the coconut milk is totally absorbed, about 15 minutes.

3. Heat the coconut oil in a small sauté pan over medium-low heat. Add the shallots and garlic and fry until golden brown, 3 to 5 minutes. Remove with a slotted spoon.

4. Pour the rice into a serving dish and sprinkle the fried shallots and garlic on top. Garnish with the cilantro.

COCONUT–CALAMANSI
LIME RICE

GLUTEN-FREE

DAIRY-FREE

This recipe is an ideal accompaniment to the Pan-Seared Halibut with Coconut Saffron Cream (page 71) as well as any Far Eastern and South Asian recipe that calls for rice as a side dish. This rice is flavored with calamansi lime juice, which is found in Asian markets, but Key lime juice is a great substitute. If you can't find either, use regular lime juice along with ½ teaspoon of grated lime zest. MAKES 4 SERVINGS

1 cup jasmine rice

1 tablespoon calamansi lime juice or Key lime juice

1 teaspoon coarse salt

1½ cups water

1 cup light coconut milk

Lime zest for garnish (optional)

1. To wash the rice, place it in a deep bowl and add enough cold water to cover by 3 inches. Swirl the rice around with your hand until the water is cloudy. Carefully drain the water. Repeat this four or five times, until the water runs clear. Set the rice aside.

2. Combine the rice, lime juice, salt, and 1½ cups water in a medium saucepan and bring to a boil. Reduce the heat to medium-high and simmer, uncovered, for 15 minutes. Remove from the heat and drain in a fine mesh sieve.

3. Return the rice to the pan and add the coconut milk. Using a spatula, smooth the rice into a high pyramid in the middle of the pot. Place a clean dish towel or doubled-up paper towels over the pot and squeeze the lid into place. Do not allow the cloth to droop over the sides; instead, fold it up over the top of the lid like a bundle. Cook the rice over low heat for 20 minutes.

4. Remove the pan from the heat and fluff the rice with a fork. Serve in a bowl. Garnish with the lime zest, if using.

JEWELED
COUSCOUS

This is one of my favorite side dishes because I find couscous to be as versatile as rice in many ways. For this recipe, I use Israeli couscous, which is the larger "pearl" variety, because it is tough enough to stand up to the addition of nuts, raisins, and curry leaves. The name for this side dish comes from a Persian rice dish that features basmati rice, pistachios, and barberries for a sweet-and-sour profile.   MAKES 4 SERVINGS

2   navel oranges or ⅓ cup dried orange peel (optional; see note)

4   cups water

½   cup sugar

2   tablespoons coconut oil

1   small red onion, thinly sliced

½   teaspoon ground cumin

½   teaspoon ground turmeric

2   cups Israeli couscous

2½ cups chicken stock or vegetable stock

1   teaspoon salt

Freshly ground black pepper

5   fresh curry leaves

⅓   cup roughly chopped cashews

⅓   cup golden raisins

⅓   cup toasted shredded coconut

Fresh parsley for garnish

recipe continues on the next page

NOTE: *Though not strictly necessary, the candied orange peel adds a wonderful flavor profile. Making your own is labor intensive but well worth it. You can purchase dried orange peel in Middle Eastern markets; make sure to purchase the long strips of orange peel rather than the grated or minced varieties.*

JEWELED
COUSCOUS

continued

1. Using a sharp paring knife, score the oranges from stem end to bottom in four sections. Carefully peel away the skin. Use your paring knife to cut away the pith (white part) on the inside of the skin, then julienne each section of peel into long strips. Discard the pith.

2. Pour 1 cup of water into a small pot and bring to a boil. Add the julienned orange peel (or the dried orange peel, if that is what you're using). Simmer for 10 to 15 minutes, then drain. Repeat two more times to ensure any bitterness is removed from the peels. Drain and set aside.

3. Combine the sugar and the remaining 1 cup water in the pot. Add the orange peels and simmer until the water is nearly totally absorbed and only a few tablespoons of syrup are left in the pan, 12 to 14 minutes. Set aside.

4. Heat 1 tablespoon of the coconut oil in a medium saucepan over medium-low heat. Add half of the onion and sauté until it is nicely golden brown, 5 to 7 minutes. Add the cumin and turmeric, mix well, and fry for 30 seconds.

5. Stir in the couscous and toss well to coat, then add the stock, salt, and pepper to taste. Bring to a simmer, then reduce the heat to low and simmer, uncovered, until all of the liquid is absorbed and the couscous is tender, 15 to 20 minutes.

6. While the couscous is cooking, make the fruit and nut mix: Heat the remaining 1 tablespoon coconut oil in a medium skillet over medium-low heat. Add the curry leaves and fry until they begin to blister and curl, 30 seconds. Add the remaining onion and fry until it begins to soften, 1 to 2 minutes. Add the cashews and fry until golden brown, 1 to 2 minutes. Add the raisins and coconut and fry for 1 to 2 minutes.

7. Add the orange peel and syrup to the fruit mixture and fry for 1 to 2 minutes longer.

8. Fluff the couscous and arrange on a platter. Gently mix in the fruit mixture. Serve hot, garnished with parsley.

COCONUT
CRAB PILAF

My inspiration for this dish comes from *crab pelau*, a dish native to the island of Tobago. Crab pelau melds East Indian and African foodways as a one-pot meal of mixed rice and chicken or, in this case, crab. Coconut milk is a standard ingredient in both versions, as is Scotch bonnet chile. I like to substitute Old Bay Seasoning for the traditional green seasoning. MAKES 8 SERVINGS

2 cups long-grain rice

1 tablespoon coconut oil

2 shallots, minced

3 garlic cloves, minced

1 teaspoon West Indian curry powder

2 cups chicken stock

1 cup coconut milk

1 small Scotch bonnet chile, minced

3 sprigs fresh thyme

1 tablespoon Old Bay Seasoning

2 teaspoons coarse salt

1½ pounds lump crabmeat

1. Preheat the oven to 350°F (180°C).

2. To wash the rice, place it in a deep bowl and add enough cold water to cover by 3 inches. Swirl the rice around with your hand until the water is cloudy. Carefully drain the water. Repeat this four or fives times, until the water runs clear. Drain the rice in a sieve or colander and set aside.

3. Heat the coconut oil in a medium iron pot or oven-safe saucepan over medium-low heat. Add the shallots and garlic and fry until the shallots begin to soften, 1 to 2 minutes. Stir in the curry powder and fry for 30 to 40 seconds longer.

4. Add the drained rice and mix very well to coat, then stir in the stock and coconut milk. Add the chile, thyme, Old Bay Seasoning, and salt. Stir well. Place in the oven, uncovered, and cook until nearly all of the liquid is absorbed, 25 to 30 minutes.

5. Remove the pot from the oven and place on low heat on the stovetop. Stir in the crabmeat and cover the pot. Cook for 5 to 7 minutes longer. Serve hot.

JAMAICAN
BAMMY
CAKES

I fell in love with bammy — a fried cake made with grated and dried yucca, salt, and water — on a research trip exploring the culinary heritage of Jamaica. I had never had it before, but something about the crispy yet creamy texture really won me over. This recipe is fairly simple. If you can't find fresh yucca (cassava), not to worry: Caribbean and Indian markets usually sell frozen grated versions of the tuber. (See page 142 for more on the history of bammy.) MAKES ABOUT 16 CAKES

1½ pounds finely grated yucca
    (defrosted if frozen)

 1 tablespoon coarse salt

 1 tablespoon sugar

 ½ cup water, or more as needed

 2 cups coconut milk

 ⅓ cup coconut oil

1. Place a large handful of grated yucca in a dishcloth (not terry) or cheesecloth and twist to squeeze out the liquid. Repeat with all of the yucca, squeezing out as much liquid as possible. Spread the yucca on a sheet pan or baking sheet, break up any lumps with a fork, and allow to dry out for at least 2 hours and up to 1 day.

2. Mix the yucca with the salt and sugar in a large bowl. Slowly add the water to create a thick doughlike batter, adding more water as needed. Set aside.

3. Place the coconut milk in a high-sided baking dish. Heat half of the coconut oil in a large nonstick skillet over medium-low heat. Add 2 to 3 tablespoons of the yucca batter to the pan. Gently press down the batter with the back of a spoon and smooth into a circle about 3 to 4 inches wide. Add more batter, 2 to 3 table-spoons for each cake, leaving about ½ inch around each bammy. Fry until golden brown, 3 to 4 minutes on each side, adding more coconut oil as necessary. You may have to fry the bammy in batches. As the bammy are done, remove them from the pan, place them in the coconut milk, and let soak for 10 to 15 minutes.

4. Remove each bammy from the coconut milk and shake or pat dry. Heat the skillet again over medium-low heat and add the remaining oil. Return the bammy to the skillet and fry until lightly golden brown, 2 to 3 minutes on each side. Serve hot.

bammy's roots

Bammy hearkens back to a staple food of the native Caribbean people, prior to Western colonization. It is most often eaten with stews or soups or with salted codfish for breakfast. In Jamaica, and in Caribbean markets, you can buy packaged bammy for soaking in coconut milk, then baking or frying, but as with anything, fresh is best.

COCONUT STICKY RICE

Coconut sticky rice is most often served as a dessert, but I like to make it as a savory dish to accompany stews or satay. Thai sticky rice, also called sweet glutinous rice, is a hard grain that needs to be soaked for many hours, so plan ahead. You'll need a bamboo steamer or a metal steamer insert lined with parchment paper. MAKES 8 SERVINGS

2 cups Thai sticky rice

1½ cups coconut milk

2 teaspoons salt

1. To wash the rice, place it in a deep bowl and add enough cold water to cover by 3 inches. Swirl the rice around with your hand until the water is cloudy. Carefully drain the water. Repeat this four or five times, until the water runs clear. Cover the rice with 4 cups of water and let soak for at least 6 hours and up to 24 hours.

2. Set a bamboo steamer or metal steamer insert in a medium saucepan. Line the steamer with parchment paper and add enough water in the bottom of the pan to come halfway up the side of the steamer.

3. Drain the rice and mound it on the parchment. Bring the water to a simmer and cover the pan. Allow the rice to steam over medium-low heat until it is tender and soft, 25 to 30 minutes.

4. Heat the coconut milk and salt in another medium saucepan over medium-low heat. Add the cooked rice and simmer, stirring constantly, until the liquid is fully absorbed, 8 to 10 minutes. Serve hot.

VARIATION: DESSERT RICE

If you'd rather make a dessert rice, simply add ¼ cup of sugar to the coconut milk in step 4 and serve with fresh, ripe mango.

YUCCA FRITES

GLUTEN-FREE

DAIRY-FREE

PALEO-FRIENDLY

Yucca frites go exceptionally well with any meal that usually calls for french fries. They are excellent accompaniments to the Ultimate Vegan Burger (page 75), Coconut-Cashew Fried Chicken (page 89), and Coconut Spareribs (page 91). These frites are crispy with a delightfully soft center. I like to liberally sprinkle mine with Himalayan pink salt. MAKES 4 SERVINGS

8 cups water

1 tablespoon salt

2 large yucca (cassava), peeled and cut in half (see note)

½ cup coconut oil

Himalayan pink salt or fleur de sel

1. Bring the water and the 1 tablespoon salt to a boil in a large deep pot. Add the yucca halves and reduce the heat to a simmer. Cook until they are just fork-tender, about 30 minutes. Do not boil the yucca to the point where it is soft enough to break apart.

2. Remove the yucca from the pot and allow to cool until the halves are easy to handle. Slice each half lengthwise and remove the fibrous center.

3. Slice the yucca pieces into thick french fries and set aside.

4. Heat the coconut oil in a large skillet over medium-high heat. Add the yucca fries in batches and fry until golden brown, 10 to 12 minutes. Remove with a slotted spoon to a sheet pan lined with paper towels or a wire rack set over a sheet pan. Sprinkle generously with the pink salt and serve hot.

NOTE: *Peeled yucca with the fibrous center removed is available in most supermarkets. If using frozen, simply simmer in water until fork tender, then slice and fry.*

5
breakfasts

To me, coconut is the ideal ingredient for breakfasts of all kinds. It can be creamy, crunchy, sweet, or savory and lends itself nicely to breakfast offerings that feature fresh, dried, or roasted fruit. This collection features my very favorite coconut breakfasts both for everyday meals and for those special occasions when you have more time to prepare. Some of the recipes, like the Coconut-Cashew-Date Breakfast Bites or the Coconut-Pineapple Granola, are also ideal snacks — perfect for making in extra batches and storing for the morning meal or whenever.

DAD'S DAILY
COCONUT BREAD

This recipe is so familiar to me that I can make it on autopilot. It is a basic quick bread recipe (like a carrot, pumpkin, or zucchini bread) but with coconut instead. You can substitute dried coconut for the fresh, but if you do so, increase the quantity of milk to 18 ounces. You can use regular milk in place of the evaporated, but the resulting bread will not be as tender. You'll find mixed essence (a blend of artificial almond, orange, and pear flavorings) in Caribbean markets.

MAKES 2 LOAVES

3 cups all-purpose flour

1 cup grated fresh or frozen coconut

1 cup sugar

1 tablespoon baking powder

1 teaspoon salt

1 (12-ounce) can evaporated milk

1 cup (2 sticks) unsalted butter, melted and cooled

1 egg

1 teaspoon mixed essence

Sugar for dusting the top of the loaves (optional)

1. Preheat the oven to 350°F (180°C).

2. Mix together the flour, coconut, sugar, baking powder, and salt in a large bowl. Set aside.

3. Beat together the milk, butter, egg, and mixed essence in another large bowl. Slowly add the flour mixture to the milk mixture and beat until well incorporated. The batter will be thick.

4. Spray two 8½- by 4½-inch loaf pans with cooking spray and fill each three-quarters full with batter. Bake for 40 to 50 minutes, or until the top is golden brown and a cake tester inserted into the center of the loaf comes out clean. Dust the top of the loaves with sugar, if using, and allow to cool slightly before unmolding. Serve warm or store in an airtight container for up to 4 days. Coconut bread may also be frozen for up to 1 month if well wrapped.

NOTE: *You can also bake the batter in muffin pans. Just reduce the baking time to 25 to 30 minutes.*

sunday bread

My father used to make this bread on special occasions, but in his home of Trinidad, this bread — with the addition of candied fruits or raisins — would be prepared in quantity on Sunday to be used for breakfast, afternoon tea, or a children's snack all week. I've readopted that custom, baking coconut bread at least twice a week to keep on hand for my family.

COCONUT
BAO

For my version of coconut *bao*, or *gai mei bao*, I adapted the savory recipe from my book *Sweet Hands: Island Cooking from Trinidad and Tobago* with a coconut filling. You'll often see these buns sprinkled with sesame seeds as a garnish, but I like to paint mine with sugar syrup and then lightly dust them with superfine grated coconut instead. A warning: coconut bao are incredibly addictive. Once you've had these breakfast pastries, your run-of-the-mill doughnut will fail to please! MAKES 20 BUNS

filling

½ cup (1 stick) unsalted butter, softened

½ cup sugar

¼ cup plus 1 tablespoon nonfat dry milk powder

¾ cup dried unsweetened shredded coconut

1 teaspoon vanilla extract

dough

2¼ teaspoons (1 packet) active dry yeast

½ cup plus 3 tablespoons plus ½ teaspoon sugar

½ cup warm water (110°F/45°C)

3 cups all-purpose flour

1¼ teaspoons baking powder

1 egg

1 egg white

1 tablespoon vegetable shortening melted with 1 tablespoon hot water

egg wash

1 egg

1 tablespoon water

garnishing syrup

¼ cup sugar

¼ cup water

1 cup dried superfine grated coconut

recipe continues on page 152

COCONUT BAO *continued*

1. To make the filling, combine the butter and sugar in a large bowl or the bowl of a stand mixer fitted with a paddle attachment. With a handheld or stand mixer, beat at medium speed until the mixture is pale yellow and fluffy, 4 to 5 minutes.

2. Add the milk powder and beat 1 minute. Add the coconut and vanilla and beat another minute. Set aside.

3. To make the dough, combine the yeast and ½ teaspoon of the sugar in a deep bowl. Add the warm water and stir well. Set aside until foamy, 1 to 2 minutes.

4. Combine the flour, baking powder, and the remaining ½ cup plus 3 tablespoons sugar in a large bowl or the bowl of a stand mixer fitted with a dough hook or paddle attachment. Add the yeast mixture, egg, egg white, and shortening mixture. Mix at high speed for 4 minutes, then at the lowest speed for 6 minutes. The dough should be smooth and soft. Test the dough by pressing it with your finger; it should leave a mark that springs back slowly. Set aside the dough to rise for 1 hour, or until doubled in size.

5. Flour a clean, dry work surface. Cut the dough into four equal pieces. With your hands, roll the pieces of dough into ropes about 3 inches in diameter and about 10 inches long. Cut each rope into five pieces. Knead each piece for 30 seconds, then form into a ball. Set the dough balls on a floured surface.

6. Flatten one ball of dough into a 4-inch disk. Spread 1 tablespoon of the coconut filling evenly down the middle of the disk. Fold the disk over the filling and pinch together the seams. Gently mold the dough into a cigar shape and place seam side down on a sheet pan lined with parchment paper. Repeat with all of the dough balls. Once all the bao are on the pan, set aside to rise for 1 hour, or until doubled in size.

7. Preheat the oven to 350°F (180°C).

8. Make the egg wash by beating together the egg and water. Brush each bao with the wash. Bake for 10 to 15 minutes, or until the bao have risen and are deeply golden brown.

9. While the bao are baking, make the garnishing syrup: Combine the sugar and water in a small saucepan and bring to a boil over medium heat. Cook until reduced to a syrup that coats the back of a spoon, 10 to 12 minutes.

10. When you've removed the bao from the oven, allow to cool for 10 minutes and then brush them lightly with the syrup. Immediately sprinkle with a fine dusting of superfine coconut. Bao may be stored in ziplock bags for up to 3 days.

traditional bao

Bao — the puffy Chinese bun stuffed with barbecued pork — is standard not only in Cantonese cuisine but also in my father's home island of Trinidad, where it is called "pow." In Trinidad, the fillings vary from pork to chicken to shrimp and vegetables, and the bakeries and restaurants that carry the cloud-like pastry usually sell out by 11:00 A.M. Coconut bao, or gai mei bao, are also called cocktail buns and are a sweet version of the Chinese breakfast classic.

GLUTEN-FREE
COCONUT BREAD
WITH MEYER LEMON GLAZE

This bread was created by my dear friend Lorilynn Bauer, a chef who was, for many seasons, Cat Cora's sous-chef on Food Network's *Iron Chef America*. This gluten-free coconut bread came about when someone asked her to create a delectable loaf bread that no one would suspect was gluten-free. This easy version, with its almost cake-like texture, fits the bill and more. MAKES 1 LOAF

bread

- ¾ cup (1½ sticks) unsalted butter, softened
- 1¾ cups sugar
- 3 eggs
- ¾ cup coconut milk
- 1 tablespoon vanilla extract
  Zest of 1 Meyer lemon or regular lemon, grated
- 2 cups all-purpose gluten-free flour
- 2 teaspoons gluten-free baking powder
- ¼ teaspoon salt
- ½ cup unsweetened shredded coconut

meyer lemon glaze

- 3 tablespoons unsalted butter
- ¼ cup lightly packed brown sugar
- 2 tablespoons coconut milk
- ½ teaspoon vanilla extract
  Juice of 1 Meyer lemon (about 3 tablespoons)
- ¼ cup toasted coconut flakes for garnish

1. Preheat the oven to 350°F (180°C).

2. Combine the butter and sugar in a large bowl or the bowl of a stand mixer fitted with a paddle attachment. Cream the butter and sugar together with a handheld or stand mixer until light and fluffy, about 4 minutes.

3. Add the eggs, one at a time, beating well after each addition. Add the coconut milk, vanilla, and lemon zest, and mix well.

4. In another large bowl, whisk together the flour, baking powder, salt, and shredded coconut. Add the flour mixture to the butter mixture and mix with a handheld or stand mixer until thoroughly combined.

5. Spray an 8- by 4-inch loaf pan with cooking spray and pour in the batter. Bake for 30 to 35 minutes, or until a cake tester inserted into the center comes out clean. Allow to cool for 10 minutes on a wire rack before turning out of the pan. Cool completely.

6. While the cake is baking, make the glaze: Combine the butter and sugar in a small saucepan over medium heat. Stir with a wooden spoon until all of the sugar melts. Remove from the heat and add the coconut milk, vanilla, and lemon juice. Mix well.

7. Spoon the glaze over the cooled cake and garnish with the toasted coconut before serving.

COCONUT-GINGER SCONES
WITH APRICOT

Here I've adapted a classic scone recipe to incorporate coconut milk and coconut flakes. This particular flavor combination is based on a bread pudding that I quickly threw together when some friends delighted us with a surprise visit, and it's become a favorite ever since. The rosewater (found in Middle Eastern and Indian grocers) and cardamom give this scone a very Persian profile, but you can omit them if you don't like them. MAKES 6 LARGE SCONES

3 cups all-purpose flour, or more as needed

¼ cup plus 1 tablespoon sugar

1 tablespoon baking powder

1 teaspoon baking soda

¾ teaspoon salt

½ teaspoon ground cardamom

½ teaspoon ground nutmeg

½ cup finely chopped dried apricots

½ cup (1 stick) cold unsalted butter, cut into pieces

¾ cup buttermilk

½ cup coconut milk

1 teaspoon vanilla extract

½ teaspoon rosewater

1. Preheat the oven to 450°F (230°C). Lightly grease a baking sheet or sheet pan, or line it with parchment paper.

2. Whisk together the flour, ¼ cup of the sugar, and the baking powder, baking soda, salt, cardamom, and nutmeg in a large bowl.

3. Stir in the apricots and then, using a pastry cutter or a fork, cut in the butter until the mixture comes together in pea-size balls. Alternatively, you can put the flour mixture in a food processor and add the butter, pulsing a few times to get this consistency. Just be sure not to overmix.

4. Mix together the buttermilk, coconut milk, vanilla, and rosewater in another bowl or a large measuring cup. Add it to the flour mixture. Use a rubber spatula or a wooden spoon to gently mix the batter until it forms a mass. Add flour as needed so the mass is not sticky but still soft and pliable.

5. Turn the dough out onto the prepared baking sheet. Form the dough into a disk about 2½ inches thick. Using a sharp knife or dough scraper, cut it into six wedges. Gently separate the wedges so they have about ½ inch of room between them.

6. Bake the scones for 10 to 15 minutes, depending on your oven, or until they are lightly golden brown. Remove from the oven and dust with the remaining 1 tablespoon sugar. Serve hot. You may store these in an airtight container for up to 3 days.

PANI POPO
BREAKFAST BUNS

If you like fluffy dinner rolls, cinnamon rolls, or sticky buns, you'll love *pani popo*. This Samoan bread is basically an egg-based dinner roll that is baked in sweetened coconut milk, so the sticky part of the bun is on the bottom. Reconstituted powdered coconut milk (King Arthur Flour makes an excellent brand for baking) works extremely well for the coconut sauce because you can control the consistency, but any good-quality, full-fat canned coconut milk works well, too. MAKES 20 BUNS

buns

- ½ cup warm milk (110°F/45°C)
- ½ cup warm water (110°F/45°C)
- 2¼ teaspoons (1 packet) active dry yeast
- ⅓ cup plus 1 teaspoon sugar
- 3¾ cups all-purpose flour, or more as needed
- ½ teaspoon salt
- ¼ cup (½ stick) unsalted butter, softened
- 1 egg
- 1 teaspoon vanilla extract
- 1 teaspoon coconut oil

sauce

- ½ cup sugar
- Water, as needed
- 8 tablespoons coconut milk powder or canned coconut milk
- 1 teaspoon coconut extract

egg wash

- 1 egg yolk
- 1 tablespoon water

1. To make the buns, combine the milk and water in a large mixing bowl or the bowl of a stand mixer and sprinkle the yeast on top. Sprinkle 1 teaspoon of the sugar over the yeast, stir, and set aside until it froths and bubbles, about 5 minutes.

2. Whisk together the flour, salt, and the remaining ⅓ cup sugar in another large bowl and set aside.

3. Add the butter, egg, and vanilla to the yeast mixture. With a handheld or stand mixer, mix at medium speed until well combined.

4. Add one-third of the flour mixture to the yeast mixture and mix at medium-low speed until combined. Add the remaining flour in two more parts and mix after each addition until combined. Continue mixing the dough until it is smooth and slightly sticky, 4 to 5 minutes, adding more flour by the tablespoon as needed to achieve this texture.

5. Oil the bowl that held the flour mixture with the coconut oil. Place the dough in the bowl, then turn it over so it is well coated. Cover the bowl and set it in a warm place for the dough to rise until doubled in size, about 1 hour, depending on the temperature of the room.

6. Remove the dough and place on a clean, lightly floured surface. Cut the dough into 20 equal pieces (weighing the pieces ensures they are equal — 1 to 1½ ounces each) and form into rolls. Grease a 9- by 13-inch baking dish. Set the rolls in the dish and cover with a clean dish towel. Set aside to rise until double in size, about 1 hour, depending on the temperature of the room.

7. To make the coconut sauce, heat the sugar and 1¼ cups of water if using coconut milk powder, or ¼ cup of water if using canned coconut milk, in a medium saucepan over medium-low heat. If using coconut milk powder, whisk the powder in a small bowl to remove any lumps, then slowly whisk it into the sugar mixture. If using canned coconut milk, pour into the saucepan. Whisk constantly until the sugar is dissolved. Remove from the heat and stir in the coconut extract. Cool slightly.

8. Preheat the oven to 350°F (180°C).

9. Beat the egg yolk with the 1 tablespoon of water in a small bowl to make an egg wash. Pour the coconut sauce over the rolls and brush each roll with the egg wash.

10. Bake the rolls for 20 to 25 minutes, or until they have risen and are deeply golden brown. The rolls will absorb the coconut sauce. Serve warm. The rolls can be kept in a tightly sealed ziplock bag for up to 3 days.

NOTE: *You can make this recipe ahead of time and freeze the formed rolls in a tightly sealed ziplock bag after the second rising. Just add a couple of hours to the in-pan rise time to ensure the rolls are doubled in size.*

samoan comfort food

Popular not only in Samoa but in New Zealand, with its large Samoan population, *pani popo* are considered one of the core comfort foods of Samoan cooking. I have to agree that there is nothing quite like one of these upside-down sticky buns with a hot cup of tea on a chilly morning.

SWEET COCONUT CRÊPES

There is little difference in the recipes for savory or sweet coconut crêpes except for the addition of sugar and the omission of savory herbs. Sweet crêpes can be filled with anything from fresh fruit to jam to Nutella, the European chocolate-hazelnut spread that has become so popular. I like to keep it simple, filling the sweet crêpes with fresh strawberries and topping them with whipped cream. MAKES 4 CRÊPES

4 egg whites

2 tablespoons coconut oil, melted, or 2 tablespoons liquid coconut oil, such as Nature's Way brand

2½ tablespoons coconut flour

¼ teaspoon salt

¼ teaspoon baking soda

½ teaspoon cornstarch

½ cup coconut milk

1 teaspoon vanilla extract

1 tablespoon sugar

¼ cup water

Chopped fruit, whipped cream, jam, confectioners' sugar, or chocolate spread for filling and topping, as desired

1. Beat the eggs and coconut oil together in a large bowl.

2. Whisk together the coconut flour, salt, baking soda, and cornstarch in a small bowl. Add to the egg mixture and stir. Add the coconut milk, vanilla, and sugar and beat well so the batter is smooth and has no clumps. Stir in the water. The batter will be thin.

3. Heat a nonstick 8-inch skillet over medium heat. Spray with cooking spray and pour 2 to 3 tablespoons of the batter into the pan. Swirl the pan so the batter evenly coats the bottom and sides.

4. Cook until the batter is crisp at the edges and bubbling in the center, about 1 minute. Flip the crêpe and cook until crisp, another 1 to 2 minutes. Repeat until all the batter is used. Set the cooked crêpes aside in a warm oven to stay hot.

5. Stuff the crêpes with fillings of your choice by spreading the filling down the middle of a crêpe and rolling up the crêpe. Dust the finished crêpe with confectioners' sugar or top with whipped cream, as desired.

SAVORY COCONUT CRÊPES
WITH EGGS, MUSHROOMS, AND GRUYÈRE CHEESE

I love crêpes because they are so versatile. They can be sweet or savory, stuffed or unstuffed. Coconut flour is, in my opinion, ideal for crêpe batter because it lacks gluten, so that nice flat crêpe consistency is created by default. These crêpes, minus the thyme, are excellent for use with the Summer Rolls (page 50).

MAKES 4 CRÊPES

crêpes

- 4 egg whites
- 2 tablespoons coconut oil, melted, or 2 tablespoons liquid coconut oil, such as Nature's Way brand
- 2½ tablespoons coconut flour
- ¼ teaspoon baking soda
- 1 teaspoon cornstarch
- ¼ teaspoon salt
- 1 teaspoon finely chopped fresh thyme
- ½ cup coconut milk
- ¼ cup water

filling

- 1 tablespoon butter
- 1 small shallot, minced
- 3 cups chopped mixed mushrooms (like baby bella, shiitake, and chanterelle)
- Salt and freshly ground black pepper
- 4 eggs
- ¼ cup milk
- 2 tablespoons chopped fresh parsley
- 6 tablespoons grated Gruyère cheese

recipe continues on the next page

SAVORY COCONUT CRÊPES *continued*

1. To make the crêpes, beat the eggs and coconut oil together in a large bowl.

2. Whisk together the coconut flour, baking soda, cornstarch, salt, and thyme in a separate bowl. Add to the egg mixture and stir. Add the coconut milk and water and beat well so the batter is smooth and has no clumps. The batter will be thin.

3. Heat a nonstick 8-inch skillet over medium heat. Spray with cooking spray and pour 2 to 3 tablespoons of the batter into the pan. Swirl the pan so the batter evenly coats the bottom and sides.

4. Cook until the batter is crisp at the edges and bubbling in the center, about 1 minute. Flip the crêpe and cook until crisp, another 1 to 2 minutes. Repeat until all the batter is used. Set the cooked crêpes aside in a warm oven to stay hot.

5. To make the filling, heat the butter in a medium skillet over medium heat. When the butter melts, add the shallot and fry until softened, 1 to 2 minutes. Add the mushrooms and fry until they are softened and reduced to about 2 cups, 5 to 10 minutes. Season with salt and pepper to taste and set aside.

6. Beat the eggs with the milk in a large bowl. Heat a large nonstick skillet over medium heat. Spray the pan with cooking spray and add the eggs. Allow the eggs to set for about 1 minute and then, using a rubber spatula, push the edges of the eggs toward the middle of the pan. Repeat all the way around the pan in order to scramble the eggs. Cook until the eggs are firm but not dry, 1 to 2 minutes.

7. Lay the crêpes on a platter. Divide the scrambled eggs and cooked mushrooms equally among them, portioning the filling down the center of each crêpe. Top with the parsley and cheese. Roll up each crêpe. Serve warm.

COCONUT BRAN MUFFINS

Although you can always bake Dad's Daily Coconut Bread (page 148) in muffin pans — and I often do — I developed this coconut muffin to include bran for its extra fiber and vitamin complex, making it a good choice for breakfast. If you want to add extra protein, you can toss in 1 tablespoon of protein powder (I like hemp seed powder). MAKES 12 MUFFINS

¾ cup milk, or more as needed

¼ cup coconut oil, melted

¼ cup plain yogurt

½ teaspoon vanilla extract

1 egg

1¼ cups all-purpose flour

1¼ cups wheat bran

¾ cup firmly packed light brown sugar

½ cup toasted grated coconut

2 tablespoons coconut flour

2 teaspoons baking powder

1 teaspoon baking soda

½ teaspoon ground cinnamon

½ teaspoon salt

1. Preheat the oven to 375°F (190°C). Line a standard 12-cup muffin pan with cupcake liners or grease lightly and then dust with flour.

2. Beat together the milk, coconut oil, yogurt, and vanilla in a large bowl. Add the egg and beat well.

3. In another large bowl, whisk together the flour, wheat bran, sugar, toasted coconut, coconut flour, baking powder, baking soda, cinnamon, and salt.

4. Slowly add the flour mixture to the wet mixture, beating well after each addition. Add more milk, in small amounts, if necessary to achieve a thick batter.

5. Divide the batter evenly among the prepared cups. Bake for 10 to 15 minutes, or until the muffins are puffed and a cake tester inserted into the center comes out clean. The muffins can be stored in an airtight container or ziplock bag for up to 3 days.

COCONUT
TROPICAL FRUIT PARFAIT

This recipe is ridiculously simple but ridiculously good. I like to use a mix of tropical fruits, but you can use a single fruit of your choice. A good way to get the ripest, tastiest tropical fruit is to buy frozen chunks, but you'll have to defrost them in a sieve set over a bowl to catch the syrup.   MAKES 4 PARFAITS

1½ cups cubed (about ½ inch) papaya, mango, kiwifruit, and strawberry

1 teaspoon vanilla extract

¼ teaspoon ground cinnamon

2 cups vanilla-flavored coconut milk yogurt

1 cup Coconut-Pineapple Granola (page 168) or store-bought granola

⅔ cup sweetened coconut flakes

1. Have four champagne flutes ready. Combine the fruits, vanilla, and cinnamon in a large bowl and mix well.

2. Spoon about ⅓ cup of the yogurt into the bottom of each flute. Top with a tablespoon of granola and then with 2 tablespoons of fruit. Repeat until each glass is filled with layers of yogurt, granola, and fruit. Garnish with the flaked coconut and serve.

COCONUT-PINEAPPLE
GRANOLA

Adding chopped dried fruit to my granola halfway through baking allows the sugar in the fruit to melt a bit and stick to the clusters after they're broken up without burning the fruit. This recipe is excellent for the Coconut Tropical Fruit Parfait on page 166, or with milk, or simply to eat out of hand.

MAKES ABOUT 1 POUND

4 cups rolled oats

¼ cup wheat germ or hemp seed powder

½ teaspoon coarse salt

½ teaspoon ground cinnamon

¼ teaspoon ground nutmeg

½ cup (1 stick) unsalted butter

½ cup coconut nectar

½ cup firmly packed light brown sugar

1 teaspoon vanilla extract

2 egg whites

1 cup large unsweetened flaked coconut, such as Bob's Red Mill brand

1 cup dried pineapple chunks, chopped into small pieces

⅔ cup macadamia nuts, coarsely chopped

1. Preheat the oven to 350°F (180°C). Lightly spray two baking sheets with cooking spray.

2. Combine the oats, wheat germ, salt, cinnamon, and nutmeg in a large bowl. Mix well and set aside.

3. Melt the butter in a medium saucepan over medium-low heat. Add the coconut nectar and brown sugar and stir until the sugar is dissolved, about 2 minutes. Remove from the heat and stir in the vanilla. Pour over the oats mixture and mix well.

4. Spread the oats mixture evenly on the prepared baking sheets. Bake for 15 minutes, stirring once halfway through cooking. Remove the oats from the oven and allow them to cool for 5 minutes. Raise the oven temperature to 400°F (200°C).

5. Pour the oats mixture into a large bowl. Mix in the egg whites, then fold in the coconut flakes, pineapple chunks, and macadamia nuts.

6. Spread the mixture back on the baking sheets and press down so it is smooth and even. Bake for 5 to 7 minutes. Turn off the oven and allow the granola to sit in the oven for 5 minutes. Then remove the granola from the oven and allow to cool completely.

7. Break the granola into clusters and store in an airtight container for up to 1 month.

COCONUT FLOUR
PANCAKES

It's pretty difficult to make a coconut flour pancake that is as fluffy and airy as a good wheat flour version. In part this is because coconut flour doesn't have gluten. The solution is to increase the leavening agents — in this case, eggs and baking soda — and to reduce the amount of sugar, which melts inside the batter and holds it down. I've also found that, as with many baking preparations, having the ingredients at room temperature really helps. MAKES 4 SERVINGS

 5 eggs (separate 2)
¾ cup buttermilk
½ cup coconut milk
 2 tablespoons coconut nectar
 1 teaspoon vanilla extract
¾ cup coconut flour
1½ teaspoons baking soda
¼ teaspoon salt
    Butter, coconut oil, or spray oil for frying
    Maple syrup or coconut nectar for serving

1. Combine 3 whole eggs, 2 egg yolks, and the buttermilk, coconut milk, coconut nectar, and vanilla in a large bowl. Beat until well combined and frothy.

2. Whisk together the coconut flour, baking soda, and salt in a medium bowl. Add the flour mixture to the egg mixture in three stages, beating well after each addition so that it is smooth. Set aside for 5 minutes.

3. Place the remaining 2 egg whites in a small bowl and whip until stiff peaks form. Fold gently into the pancake batter.

4. Heat a griddle or cast-iron skillet over medium-low heat. Grease with a little butter or coconut oil or spray with cooking spray.

5. Pour the batter onto the griddle or skillet and smooth into 4-inch-wide, ¼-inch-thick circles, using the bottom of a ladle or the back of a spoon. Allow ½ inch of space around each pancake.

6. Fry the pancakes until holes form in the top and they look a bit dry, 2 to 3 minutes. Flip the pancakes and cook on the other side for 2 to 3 minutes. Serve with maple syrup or coconut nectar.

SRI LANKAN HOPPERS
WITH EGG CURRY

Hoppers, or *appam*, are a staple of the Sri Lankan diet. They come in various forms, the most common being this type, a thin bowl-shaped crêpe with an egg curry or other topping that is most often eaten at breakfast. Because the hopper batter needs to ferment, it has to sit at room temperature overnight, making it a dish you have to plan for (but it's well worth the wait!). MAKES 4 SERVINGS

hoppers

- 1 teaspoon active dry yeast
- 1 tablespoon plus 1 teaspoon sugar
- 1 cup warm water (110°F/45°C), or more as needed
- 1 cup rice flour
- ¼ teaspoon salt
- 1 cup coconut milk, at room temperature
- Coconut oil for frying

egg curry

- 1 tablespoon coconut oil
- 1 shallot, minced
- 5 fresh curry leaves
- ½ teaspoon Maldive fish flakes or fermented shrimp paste
- ½ teaspoon chili powder
- ½ teaspoon ground cumin
- ½ teaspoon ground turmeric
- 1 green chile, minced
- 1 cup coconut milk
- 1 small cinnamon stick
- 6 hard-boiled eggs, sliced in half lengthwise
- 1 teaspoon salt

recipe continues on the next page

SRI LANKAN HOPPERS *continued*

1. To make the hopper batter, stir together the yeast, 1 teaspoon of the sugar, and ¼ cup of the warm water in a large bowl. Let sit until the mixture begins to foam and bubble, about 2 minutes.

2. Stir in the rice flour, salt, and the remaining ¾ cup water and mix well until the batter is smooth. Set aside to rise in a warm spot, covered with plastic wrap, overnight. It should double in size.

3. To make the egg curry, heat 1 tablespoon coconut oil in a medium saucepan over medium-low heat. Add the shallot and fry until it begins to soften, 1 minute. Add the curry leaves and fry until they begin to blister, 30 to 40 seconds, then stir in the fish flakes and fry, stirring, for 1 minute. Stir in the chili powder, cumin, turmeric, and green chile, and fry for 30 seconds.

4. Add the coconut milk and cinnamon stick, bring to a simmer, and cook until the mixture begins to thicken, about 10 minutes. Add the hard-boiled eggs and the salt and simmer 10 minutes longer.

5. While the curry is cooking, fry the hoppers: Mix the coconut milk and the remaining 1 tablespoon sugar into the risen batter. The batter should be thinner than pancake batter. Add lukewarm water, as needed, to achieve this consistency.

6. Heat a small wok over medium-low heat and brush with coconut oil. Pour about ¼ cup of batter into the pan and swirl it around so the batter thinly coats the bottom and sides of the pan. Cover the pan, allow the crêpe to cook for 1 minute, then gently remove from the pan. Repeat with all of the batter. Serve hot with egg curry spooned into the center of the hopper.

COCONUT OATMEAL
WITH ROASTED STONE FRUITS

This is a favorite late-summer breakfast of mine. I cook my oatmeal with coconut milk and then top it with the roasted stone fruits that are so plentifully in season. I top the oatmeal with granola (either homemade or store-bought) to add crunch to the dish. MAKES 4–6 SERVINGS

oatmeal

- 3 cups water
- Pinch of salt
- 2 cups rolled oats
- ½ cup coconut milk
- 2 tablespoons granulated sugar

fruit

- 2 plums, halved, pitted, and chopped into large chunks
- 2 peaches, halved, pitted, and chopped into large chunks
- ½ teaspoon ground cinnamon
- 3 tablespoons coconut sugar

finishing

- 1 cup granola
- Coconut nectar, as desired

1. To make the oatmeal, bring the water and salt to a boil in a medium saucepan. Add the oats and reduce the heat to a simmer. Cook until the water is almost completely absorbed, 5 to 7 minutes. Add the coconut milk and granulated sugar and continue to simmer, stirring often, until the coconut milk is reduced by half, about 4 minutes. Remove from the heat.

2. To roast the fruit, preheat the oven broiler and lightly coat a baking dish with cooking spray. Toss the plums and peaches in a medium bowl with the cinnamon and coconut sugar. Spread in the prepared baking dish and broil until the fruit begins to brown, 3 to 5 minutes. Remove from the oven.

3. To finish, divide the oatmeal equally among four to six bowls. Top each bowl with a portion of granola. Spoon the roasted fruit over the granola and drizzle lightly with coconut nectar.

SERABI
(INDONESIAN COCONUT PANCAKES)

These little pancakes are a popular Indonesian street food and are topped with both sweet and savory ingredients. This, the most common version, is drizzled with a sauce made from coconut milk and coconut sugar. MAKES 20-25 PANCAKES

serabi

1½ cups rice flour

1 cup finely grated fresh or frozen coconut

½ teaspoon salt

2½ cups coconut milk

sauce

2 cups coconut milk

¾ cup coconut sugar

¼ teaspoon salt

1 teaspoon vanilla extract

Bananas, strawberries, or other fruit for garnish

1. Combine the rice flour, coconut, and salt in a large bowl. Add the coconut milk and mix well until the batter is smooth and has almost no lumps (except for bits of coconut).

2. Heat a skillet or griddle over medium heat and spray with cooking spray. Using a small ladle, spoon out the batter onto the hot surface and, using the back of the ladle, smooth into a 3-inch-wide circle. Cook until the surface of the pancake is bubbled and dry looking, 1 to 2 minutes, then remove from the heat. Do not flip the serabi. Repeat until all of the batter is used.

3. To make the sauce, combine the coconut milk, coconut sugar, and salt in a medium saucepan over medium-low heat. Cook, stirring constantly, until the sugar is dissolved, about 1 minute. Simmer for 5 to 10 minutes, so that the mixture thickens slightly, and then add the vanilla. Remove from the heat and cool completely.

4. Serve by placing four or five serabi on a plate and pouring some of the coconut sauce over them. Top with fresh fruit of your choice.

traditional serabi sauce

In Indonesia, the serabi sauce is often flavored with pandan leaves, which come from a tropical plant in the screw pine family. Pandan leaves impart a citric herbaceous flavor to the pancakes and a brilliant green hue. Just as often, though, the pandan is omitted, which I've chosen to do in my serabi recipe, opting instead for vanilla as the main flavoring agent.

COCONUT
BELGIAN
WAFFLES I

This first version of Belgian waffles features coconut flour, which has a lovely, slightly sweet coconut aroma and fine powdery texture. You'll find that this dough is quite thick, almost like a quick bread, but that's okay. It's the nature of coconut flour to absorb a great deal of liquid. MAKES 4 SERVINGS

1 cup all-purpose flour

⅓ cup coconut flour

2 tablespoons sugar

1 tablespoon baking powder

1 tablespoon baking soda

⅛ teaspoon ground cardamom

⅛ teaspoon ground nutmeg

½ teaspoon salt

1 cup milk

1 cup water

¼ cup vegetable oil

1 teaspoon vanilla extract

1 teaspoon coconut extract

4 egg whites

Tropical Fruit Compote (page 178), maple syrup, or coconut nectar for serving

1. Preheat your waffle maker according to the manufacturer's directions.

2. Whisk together the flours, sugar, baking powder, baking soda, cardamom, nutmeg, and salt in a large bowl. Set aside.

3. Combine the milk, water, oil, vanilla, and coconut extract in another large bowl and mix well.

4. Slowly add the dry ingredients to the wet, mixing well to achieve a thick batter. If the batter is too dry, add a little more water in stages as needed. The batter should be fairly thick.

5. Whip the egg whites in a medium bowl until stiff peaks form. Fold the egg whites into the batter until thoroughly combined.

6. Pour about ½ cup of batter into each chamber of the waffle maker or follow the manufacturer's directions regarding volume. Bake for 5 minutes or according to the manufacturer's directions.

7. Serve the finished waffles with Tropical Fruit Compote, maple syrup, or coconut nectar.

COCONUT BELGIAN WAFFLES, II

I've included this second version of Belgian waffles for those who like just a hint of coconut flavor and texture but are otherwise waffle purists. Essentially, this recipe simply adds sweetened shredded coconut to a classic Belgian waffle batter and no more. MAKES 4 SERVINGS

2 cups all-purpose flour

½ cup dried sweetened shredded coconut

¼ cup sugar

1½ tablespoons baking powder

½ teaspoon salt

2 cups milk or buttermilk

¼ cup (½ stick) unsalted butter, melted

¼ cup vegetable oil

2 eggs, separated

1 teaspoon vanilla extract

Confectioners' sugar

Freshly cut fruit, maple syrup, and whipped cream for serving (optional)

1. Preheat your waffle maker according to the manufacturer's directions.

2. Whisk together the flour, coconut, sugar, baking powder, and salt in a large bowl. Set aside.

3. Combine the milk, butter, oil, egg yolks, and vanilla in another large bowl and beat well.

4. Slowly add the dry ingredients to the wet, whisking the whole time so there are no lumps. Another option is to mix all the liquid ingredients together in a high-powered blender, then add the dry ingredients and mix at high speed for 30 to 40 seconds to thoroughly combine into a thick smooth batter.

5. Whip the egg whites until stiff peaks form. Gently fold them into the batter.

6. Pour about ½ cup of batter into each chamber of the waffle maker or follow the manufacturer's directions regarding volume. Bake for 5 minutes or according to the manufacturer's directions.

7. Dust the finished waffles with confectioners' sugar. Serve with maple syrup or whipped cream and fruit, if desired.

TROPICAL FRUIT
COMPOTE

GLUTEN-FREE

DAIRY-FREE

PALEO-FRIENDLY

This is an incredibly versatile fruit compote, mainly because it has sweet and savory elements. You can always select frozen fruit if you cannot find fresh, and often the frozen is riper and sweeter. I have used this compote for everything from a garnish on grilled fish and other meats to a topping on Brie cheese with crackers to a simple spread on bread.

MAKES 2 CUPS

1 tablespoon coconut oil

1 garlic clove, minced

1 small shallot, minced

¼ teaspoon madras curry powder

½ cup chopped pineapple

½ cup chopped mango

½ cup chopped guava

¼ teaspoon red pepper flakes

½ teaspoon salt

1 sprig fresh thyme

1 teaspoon coconut sugar

¼ cup guava juice

¼ cup lemon juice

¼ cup water

1. Heat the coconut oil in a medium saucepan over medium heat. Add the garlic and shallot and fry until the shallot begins to soften, about 1 minute.

2. Add the curry powder and fry for 30 seconds. Then add the pineapple, mango, and guava, stir well, and fry for 1 minute longer.

3. Mix in the pepper flakes, salt, thyme, and coconut sugar, and stir until the sugar dissolves.

4. Add the guava juice, lemon juice, and water. Bring to a simmer, then reduce the heat to low and simmer until there is no visible liquid, about 5 minutes. Serve hot, or cool and store in the refrigerator for up to 2 weeks.

LOCO MOCO

Loco Moco is one of the many creative dishes born from the mixed culture that is Hawaii (see page 182). Traditionally, it is a mound of rice, a hamburger, and an over-easy egg with white gravy. My Loco Moco uses Coconut–Calamansi Lime Rice (page 135) and a seasoned mixed-meat patty as well as a curry-coconut gravy instead of the white gravy. This is an extremely filling dish that gives "big American breakfast" a whole new meaning, so bring your appetite! MAKES 4 SERVINGS

patties

- ½ pound lean ground beef
- ½ pound lean ground pork
- 2 scallions, minced
- 1 garlic clove, grated
- 1 tablespoon grated fresh ginger
- ½ teaspoon salt
  Freshly ground black pepper

gravy

- 1 cup coconut milk
- 1 tablespoon Thai red curry paste

finishing

- 4 eggs
- 4 cups Coconut–Calamansi Lime Rice (page 135)
  Minced chives for garnish

1. To make the patties, combine the beef, pork, scallions, garlic, ginger, salt, and a generous grind of pepper in a large bowl and knead well. Form into four equal-size patties.

2. Heat a large skillet over medium-high heat and add the patties. Brown on one side, 8 to 9 minutes, then flip and brown on the other side, 8 to 9 minutes longer.

3. To make the gravy, heat the coconut milk and red curry paste in a small saucepan over medium-low heat. Simmer until thickened and reduced by one-third, 5 to 7 minutes. Set aside over low heat to keep warm, but whisk before using.

4. To finish, heat a large nonstick skillet over medium-low heat and spray with cooking spray. Gently crack each egg into the pan, leaving room around them, and fry until their whites are set, 2 to 3 minutes. Gently flip the eggs over and cook for 1 minute longer. The center should remain soft.

5. Divide the rice among four plates or large bowls and place the cooked burger on top. Place an egg on top of each burger and then divide the gravy equally over the eggs. Garnish with the chives. Serve hot.

the history of loco moco

Loco Moco (*loco* is Portuguese and Hawaiian pidgin for "crazy," and *moco* is just a convenient rhyme) was created sometime in the late 1940s in a diner in Hawaii catering to high school football players who wanted something other than the sandwiches or traditional saimin noodles the shop served. They came up with a crazy idea for mounding rice, hamburger, and an over-easy egg together with gravy for a hearty and filling dish. While it may seem like a mess of ingredients — like Hawaii's famous "plate lunch" — it is surprisingly delicious.

COCONUT-CASHEW-DATE
BREAKFAST BITES

GLUTEN-FREE

DAIRY-FREE

This vegan breakfast or quick snack is filled with protein. The protein comes from nuts, nut butter, and protein powder, the last of which you can omit if you like. The sweetness comes from dates alone. Be forewarned — these bars are sticky! You'll want to wrap them in waxed paper to store or you'll have a globby mess on your hands. MAKES 9 BARS

1 cup pitted dates

1 cup unsalted cashews

4 tablespoons vegan gluten-free protein powder, such as hemp protein (optional)

½ teaspoon vanilla extract

½ teaspoon ground cinnamon

⅛ teaspoon salt

¾ cup cashew butter

1 cup unsweetened coconut flakes

1. Combine the dates, cashews, protein powder (if using), vanilla, cinnamon, and salt in a food processor and process until they form a coarse meal.

2. Transfer the date mixture to a bowl. Stir in the cashew butter. Stir well — it will be sticky.

3. Add the coconut and mix until incorporated.

4. Spread the bar mixture into a lightly greased 8-inch square pan and use a rubber spatula to press the mixture evenly into the pan. Slice into nine bars and remove from the pan. Store the bars in an airtight container in single layers with a piece of waxed paper between each layer. The bars may be stored for 1 week.

6
desserts

For many years, the only dishes on the American table that contained coconut were desserts, and with good reason. Coconut's naturally sweet taste enhances baked goods and pies without being overwhelming. Even in those international cuisines where coconut is used as a staple ingredient for savory as well as sweet dishes, the repertoire of coconut-based desserts is astonishing. As such, you'll find a prodigious number of coconut dessert recipes in this book — practically enough to be a book on its own! Those readers familiar with coconut in cakes and pies will be most accustomed to seeing flaked and sweetened coconut, but in this section you'll find the fruit makes an appearance in all its forms, from milk to cream, manna, molasses, and oil.

TOOLUM

Toolum is an old-school Trinidadian molasses candy. It is like a soft caramel, but with a more intense flavor thanks to the molasses. Its other main ingredients are coconut, dried orange peel (available in Middle Eastern markets, gourmet markets, and online), and ginger. A word of caution: the caramelized sugar in this recipe is extremely hot. Do not attempt to touch it with anything but your wooden spoon! MAKES ABOUT 18 PIECES

1 cup firmly packed light brown sugar

1 tablespoon water

1½ cups grated fresh or frozen coconut

¼ cup molasses

1½ teaspoons minced dried orange peel

1½ teaspoons grated fresh ginger

½ cup granulated sugar, or more as needed

1. Combine the brown sugar and water in a large skillet over medium-low heat. Mix and allow the sugar to melt and bubble until it reaches a deep reddish-brown color, 8 to 10 minutes.

2. Add the coconut to the caramelized sugar and mix well with a wooden spoon. Stir in the molasses and mix until well incorporated.

3. Stir in the orange peel and ginger and mix well. Cook for 3 to 4 minutes or until the mixture is thick and not runny.

4. Butter or grease a sheet pan. Spoon heaping teaspoonsful of the toolum mixture (about the size of a small chocolate truffle) about ½ inch apart onto the prepared pan. Allow the toolum to cool until it can be easily handled.

5. Place the granulated sugar in a small bowl. Drop a piece of toolum in the sugar. Pick it up and roll it between your palms into a ball. Store toolum in an airtight container, with waxed paper between the layers, for up to 2 weeks.

classic caribbean candy

In Trinidad, toolum candy is made at home and in small stores called "parlors" or "snackettes." It's hard to find toolum anymore, but it is a lovely classic Caribbean candy in the way that saltwater taffy and fudge are American heritage sweets. Toolum should normally be about the size of a golf ball, but I find that truffle-size toolum are just right.

SUGAR CAKES

Sugar cakes are a common dessert in Trinidad and Guyana. Nothing more than sugar and coconut cooked together in water until they reach a syrupy consistency and then mounded on parchment paper to dry, sugar cakes are an incredibly sweet, simple treat. Because they are so sweet, I use a 1-tablespoon cookie scoop to measure out the mixture, because that makes a manageable two-bite "cake." Note that this recipe must be made in a skillet, to aid evaporation. MAKES ABOUT 24 PIECES

2 cups finely grated fresh coconut

1 cup sugar

1 (½-inch) piece fresh ginger, peeled

1 small cinnamon stick

1 cup water

1 teaspoon coconut extract

1 teaspoon vanilla extract or mixed essence (see page 148)

1. Combine the coconut, sugar, ginger, cinnamon stick, and water in a medium skillet over medium-low heat. Bring the mixture to a boil, stirring often to melt the sugar, and cook until the mixture bubbles and clumps together, 12 to 13 minutes. There should not be any syrup visible and the coconut flakes should be translucent.

2. Take the pan off the heat and remove and discard the cinnamon stick and ginger. Stir in the coconut extract and vanilla.

3. Line a sheet pan with parchment paper. Spray a 1-tablespoon cookie scoop or a tablespoon with cooking spray. This will help keep the mixture from sticking.

4. Scoop out tablespoon-size portions of the coconut mixture and place on the parchment. The mixture will be quite hot, so don't touch it. You should have 20 to 24 pieces of candy.

5. Allow the sugar cakes to dry, uncovered, until they are firm and hard, about 24 hours. Store in a covered container for up to 1 month.

VARIATION: COLORFUL SUGAR CAKES

Those who know sugar cakes will be accustomed to seeing them in various pastel colors — mostly pink and green. I don't include food coloring in my recipe, but if you'd like to try it, use about two drops of food coloring for this amount of batter.

COCONUT
MARSHMALLOWS

I'm generally not a fan of marshmallows, finding them too sweet for my liking, but these are a pleasant variation on the sweet fluff thanks to the crunch of the toasted coconut. Because I use coconut sugar along with granulated sugar, you'll find that the marshmallows are a café au lait color, which I rather enjoy. Stacked in pretty cookie bags, between pieces of parchment paper, they make a nice holiday gift or party favor. MAKES ABOUT 24 PIECES

2 cups sweetened coconut flakes

1 cup water

1 ounce gelatin powder

1 cup granulated sugar

1 cup coconut sugar

1 cup light corn syrup

¼ teaspoon salt

2 teaspoons coconut extract

1 cup confectioners' sugar

1. Preheat the oven to 350°F (180°C).

2. Spread the coconut flakes on a baking sheet or sheet pan. Bake for 5 to 7 minutes, or until the coconut is lightly golden brown. Remove from the oven and set aside to cool.

3. Place ½ cup of the water in a large bowl or stand mixer and sprinkle with the gelatin. Let this mixture sit until the gelatin "blooms" and totally absorbs the water, 10 to 15 minutes. Set aside.

4. Combine the remaining ½ cup water with the granulated sugar, coconut sugar, corn syrup, and salt in a medium saucepan over medium-low heat. Bring the mixture to a simmer and allow it to cook until all of the sugar dissolves, 4 to 5 minutes.

5. Reduce the heat to low and continue to simmer the sugar mixture, uncovered, until a candy thermometer reaches 240°F (116°C), 20 to 25 minutes, stirring often so that the mixture doesn't boil over. If you do not have a candy thermometer, you can test whether the syrup is ready by scooping up ¼ teaspoon with a spoon and dropping it into cold water. If it forms a soft ball, then the syrup is ready.

6. Using a handheld mixer or a stand mixer with a balloon whisk attachment, mix the gelatin at medium-high speed. Slowly pour the candy syrup into the bowl with the beater going. Beat until the mixture becomes thick, white, and fluffy, 10 to 12 minutes. Stir in the coconut extract and beat for another 30 to 40 seconds.

7. Sprinkle the confectioners' sugar evenly into a 9- by 13-inch baking dish. Spray a rubber spatula lightly with cooking spray and use it to scrape the marshmallow mixture out of the mixing bowl. Spread the mixture evenly on top of the confectioners' sugar in the baking dish. Spray the rubber spatula again, as needed, to prevent the marshmallow from sticking.

8. Press the toasted coconut flakes evenly into the top of the marshmallow. Leave the dish on the counter, uncovered, for 8 hours or overnight so the marshmallows dry and set. Once set, slice them into 2-inch squares and serve.

VARIATION: COCONUT-GINGER MARSHMALLOWS

For a kick of ginger, add ¼ teaspoon ground ginger when you add the coconut extract in step 6. Instead of toasting the coconut, process the coconut flakes with 2 tablespoons candied ginger in a food processor until the mixture is like coarse sand, 30 to 40 seconds. Top the finished marshmallows with the coconut-ginger mixture.

COCONUT-CARAMEL-
CHOCOLATE
SHORTBREADS

In this version of the highly addictive Samoa Girl Scout cookie, I use coconut shortbread for the base cookie rather than plain shortbread. If you aren't up to making your own caramel, you can melt 12 ounces of soft caramel candy by heating it for 1 to 2 minutes in a microwave. If you're making your own caramel, I suggest preparing it after the cookies have been baked and fully cooled, as you will have to work quickly with the completed caramel so it does not harden. MAKES 30 COOKIES

shortbread

- 3 cups all-purpose flour
- 1 teaspoon coarse salt
- 1 cup grated fresh coconut
- 1 cup (2 sticks) unsalted butter, softened
- ½ cup sugar
- 1 egg

caramel

- ½ cup (1 stick) unsalted butter, cut into pieces
- ½ cup heavy cream
- ¼ cup light corn syrup
- 3 tablespoons water
- 1 cup sugar

topping

- 1 (12-ounce) bag semisweet chocolate chips
- 2 cups toasted shredded or grated coconut

make the shortbread

1. Sift together the flour and salt in a large bowl. Mix in the coconut.

2. In another large bowl, cream the butter and sugar with an electric mixer until fluffy, about 4 minutes. Add the egg and beat well.

3. Add the flour mixture to the butter mixture and mix well to form a smooth dough. Wrap the dough in plastic wrap and chill in the refrigerator for 1 hour.

4. Preheat the oven to 325°F (165°C).

5. Roll out the dough into a 9- by 13-inch rectangle about ½ inch thick. Slice the dough lengthwise into five equal slices, and then crosswise into six equal slices. This will give you 30 pieces of shortbread. Arrange the shortbread on an ungreased baking sheet, leaving 1 inch of space between cookies.

6. Bake the cookies for about 25 minutes, or until golden brown. Remove from the pan and place on wire racks until thoroughly cool, about 20 minutes.

make the caramel

7. Heat the butter and cream in a small saucepan over low heat until just melted and combined, 3 to 4 minutes. Remove from the heat.

8. Combine the corn syrup and the water in a medium saucepan over medium-low heat, then add the sugar. Using a wooden spoon, stir just until the sugar is moistened and resembles wet sand. Then increase the heat to medium-high and bring the mixture to a boil for 1 to 2 minutes. Cover the pan and boil for 1 minute longer. This will add moisture to the pan.

9. Remove the lid and continue to boil the mixture until it reaches 320°F (160°C) on a candy thermometer or the edges of the mixture in the pan begin to look light brown, 6 to 7 minutes.

10. Slowly add the butter mixture, stirring well and cooking until the mixture reaches 240°F (116°C). Set aside. You can store the caramel in a covered, airtight glass bowl at room temperature for up to 3 days before using. If you don't use it right away, you may have to warm the caramel slightly in the microwave (30 seconds to 1 minute on medium) before you'll be able to drizzle it over the cookies.

assemble the cookies

11. Place the chocolate chips in a large glass bowl and heat in the microwave for 1 minute. Remove from the microwave and mix well with a rubber spatula. If all of the chips are not completely melted, heat for 1 minute longer.

12. Line a baking sheet with parchment paper or a silicone pad. Dip the bottom of each piece of cooled shortbread into the melted chocolate and then place the cookies, chocolate side down, on the prepared baking sheet.

13. Using a tablespoon, scoop out the soft caramel and drizzle it evenly over the top of each cookie to coat completely.

14. Sprinkle the toasted coconut lightly but evenly over the top of the caramel. Using a clean spoon, drizzle thin lines of melted chocolate over the top of each cookie. Allow to cool until the chocolate base hardens completely.

COCONUT-ORANGE
SHORTBREAD

I love this orange-redolent version of shortbread — you'll find that it is particularly good as a tea cookie. While the sanding sugar garnish is optional, it makes for a pretty cookie that is ideal for a holiday cookie swap or to serve to guests. MAKES ABOUT 30 PIECES

3 cups all-purpose flour

1 teaspoon coarse salt

1 cup grated fresh or frozen coconut

½ cup grated orange zest

1 cup (2 sticks) unsalted butter, softened

½ cup sugar

1 egg

1 teaspoon coconut extract

1 teaspoon orange extract

Sanding sugar for garnish (optional)

1. Sift together the flour and salt in a large bowl. Mix in the coconut and the orange zest.

2. Combine the butter and sugar in another large bowl and cream with an electric mixer until fluffy, about 4 minutes. Add the egg, coconut extract, and orange extract, and beat well.

3. Add the flour mixture to the butter mixture and blend well to form a smooth dough. Wrap the dough in plastic wrap and chill in the refrigerator for 1 hour.

4. Preheat the oven to 325°F (165°C).

5. Roll out the dough into a 9- by 13-inch rectangle about ½ inch thick. Slice the dough lengthwise into five equal slices, and then crosswise into six equal slices. This will give you 30 pieces of shortbread. Arrange on an ungreased baking sheet, leaving 1 inch of space between cookies. Evenly dust each cookie with the sanding sugar, if using.

6. Bake the cookies for about 25 minutes, or until golden brown. Remove from the pan and place on wire racks until thoroughly cool, about 20 minutes.

fun with shapes

I like to experiment with different shapes of cookie cutters to add elegance or whimsy to the final product. Star-shaped cutters make these cookies a nice addition to a holiday cookie swap, while bars or rounds create more of an everyday cookie. The ambitious baker will find that this cookie is also suitable for "cutout"-style sandwich cookies, in which a top cookie with a pattern punched out of the middle is laid over a solid cookie that has been coated with caramel or orange marmalade, then the top of the finished cookie is drizzled with melted chocolate and toasted coconut.

AUSTRALIAN
LAMINGTONS

Lamingtons — squares of cake dipped in chocolate and then rolled in shredded coconut — are one of the most beloved desserts in Australia. For this version, I use a basic sturdy yellow cake recipe to which I've added coconut extract and a bit of coconut milk to boost the coconut flavor. In place of the traditional supersweet glaze of milk chocolate or a milk chocolate frosting, I use a simple bittersweet chocolate ganache that hardens nicely and makes the eating a shade less messy. MAKES ABOUT 16 PIECES

cake

- ½ cup (1 stick) unsalted butter, softened
- 1 cup sugar
- 2 eggs
- 1 teaspoon coconut extract
- 1 teaspoon vanilla extract
- 2 teaspoons baking powder
- 1 teaspoon baking soda
- 1⅔ cups cake flour, sifted
- 1 teaspoon salt
- 1 cup buttermilk

chocolate ganache

- 1½ cups heavy cream
- 12 ounces bittersweet chocolate, finely chopped
- 2–3 cups dried unsweetened finely grated coconut

1. Preheat the oven to 350°F (180°C). Line an 8-inch square baking pan with a piece of parchment paper. Spray the parchment and the sides of the pan with cooking spray.

2. To make the cake, combine the butter and sugar in a large bowl or the bowl of a stand mixer fitted with a paddle attachment. Using a handheld or stand mixer, cream until fluffy, 4 to 5 minutes.

3. Add the eggs one at a time, beating well after each addition. Beat the whole mixture until light and fluffy, 2 to 3 minutes.

4. Stir in the coconut extract, vanilla, baking powder, and baking soda.

5. Whisk together the flour and salt in a small bowl. Add one-third of the flour to the butter mixture and beat well. Then add one-third of the buttermilk and beat well. Repeat, alternating the flour and buttermilk, until totally combined.

6. Pour the batter into the prepared pan. Bake for 30 to 40 minutes, or until the cake is golden brown and beginning to pull away from the pan and a cake tester inserted into the center comes out clean. Allow to cool for 10 minutes in the pan on a wire rack, then flip it out onto the rack to cool completely (see note).

recipe continues on the next page

NOTE: *I find that freezing the cake before cutting makes it easier to coat the pieces in ganache and coconut.*

AUSTRALIAN LAMINGTONS

continued

7. Slice the cooled cake into 2-inch squares. You should have about 16 pieces.

8. To make the chocolate ganache, heat the cream in a medium saucepan over low heat. When bubbles begin to form at the edges of the pan, add the chocolate and cook, whisking constantly, until completely melted. Remove from the heat.

9. Place the grated coconut in a wide dish. Line a tray with parchment or waxed paper. Spear each cake square with a fork and dip into the ganache so that it is totally coated. Gently scrape off the excess with a rubber spatula or allow it to drip off, then place the cake square in the coconut and turn so all sides are coated. Place the finished Lamingtons on the prepared tray.

10. Allow the coated squares to cool completely before serving. Lamingtons may be stored in an airtight container in a single layer for 3 days.

the ubiquitous lamington

Lamingtons are named after the nineteenth-century governor of Australia, Lord Lamington. Lamingtons are sold in every pastry shop, grocer, and corner market in Australia. They are as ubiquitous at bake sales in that country as cupcakes are here in America.

MEXICAN WEDDING COOKIES
WITH COCONUT

This recipe is a riff on the Mexican wedding cookies called *polavarones*, which feature ground walnuts and a liberal dusting of confectioners' sugar (*polvo* is Spanish for "powdered"). In this version of the Christmastime favorite, I've reduced the standard measure of nuts and replaced some of it with dried coconut. MAKES ABOUT 48 COOKIES

1 cup (2 sticks) unsalted butter, softened

½ cup confectioners' sugar, plus more for garnish

½ teaspoon vanilla extract

½ teaspoon coconut extract

2 cups all-purpose flour

¼ teaspoon salt

½ cup chopped walnuts

¼ cup toasted grated coconut

1. Combine the butter and sugar in a large bowl or the bowl of a stand mixer fitted with a paddle attachment. Using a handheld or stand mixer, cream the butter and sugar at medium speed until fluffy, about 4 minutes.

2. Add the vanilla and coconut extract and beat well.

3. Whisk together the flour and salt in another large bowl. Add to the butter mixture and mix at medium speed until totally combined.

4. Combine the walnuts and coconut in a food processor and process until the mixture is the texture of coarse sand. Add these to the butter mixture and mix until they are just thoroughly combined. Wrap the dough in plastic wrap and chill in the refrigerator for 20 minutes.

5. Preheat the oven to 325°F (165°C). Line a baking sheet with parchment paper.

6. Using a 1-tablespoon cookie scoop or a tablespoon, scoop out balls of dough and place them on the prepared baking sheet. If you are using a tablespoon, gently roll the dough into a ball, but do not overhandle or you will melt the butter in the dough.

7. Bake for 14 to 15 minutes, or until just golden brown on top. Allow the cookies to cool on the baking sheet for 5 minutes.

8. Spoon some confectioners' sugar into a small handheld sieve and shake the sugar over the cookies until they are completely coated.

CARIBBEAN
COCONUT
TURNOVERS

Handheld pies that hail from the English tradition of the "pasty" remain popular in the Caribbean, the most famous perhaps being Jamaican beef patties. Coconut-filled turnovers are a heritage pastry that were most often made at home for special occasions. Similar in appearance to a Mexican empanada, these little turnovers are a lovely alternative to apple or peach turnovers for the coconut lover. MAKES 15–20 TURNOVERS

pastry

2 cups all-purpose flour, or more as needed

Pinch of coarse or kosher salt

¾ cup (1½ sticks) cold unsalted butter, diced

Ice water, as needed

filling

1 cup water

2½ cups grated fresh or frozen coconut

¾ cup sugar

1 cinnamon stick

1 teaspoon vanilla extract

⅛ teaspoon ground allspice

1 egg, beaten

1. Mix together the flour and salt in a large bowl. Cut in the butter with a pastry cutter or two knives until the dough reaches the consistency of coarse meal with pea-size pieces. Alternatively, combine the flour, salt, and butter in a food processor fitted with a plastic blade and pulse quickly. Do not overwork the dough. If using a food processor, remove the dough from the machine at this point and place in a mixing bowl. Using a spoon, stir the dough while adding drops of ice water until the dough just comes together in a ball.

2. Wrap the dough in plastic wrap and flatten to form a disk. Refrigerate for at least 2 hours, or as long as overnight. The dough may also be frozen and then thawed in the refrigerator.

3. To make the filling, combine the water, coconut, sugar, and cinnamon stick in a large skillet over medium-high heat. Bring the mixture to a simmer, stirring often, and cook until the sugar dissolves and a thick syrup forms. Continue to cook until there is almost no liquid remaining, 10 to 11 minutes total.

4. Remove from the heat. Remove and discard the cinnamon stick. Stir in the vanilla and allspice and mix well. Set aside to cool completely.

5. Remove the dough from the refrigerator. Dust a work surface and a rolling pin with flour. Roll out the pastry ⅛ inch thick, sprinkling with additional flour as necessary to keep the dough from sticking. Use a pastry brush to dust away any excess flour. Cut circles from the dough using a 5-inch round pastry cutter.

6. Place 1 to 2 tablespoons of the coconut mixture in the center of each round. Brush the edges of the pastry with the beaten egg and fold over the filling. Use a fork to crimp the edges of each pastry closed.

7. Brush the top of each pastry with the remaining egg. Using a fork, poke a few air vents in the top of each turnover.

8. Preheat the oven to 425°F (220°C).

9. Place the turnovers on an ungreased baking sheet and refrigerate for 15 minutes so that the butter in the crust becomes firm (once baked, the butter will melt and release steam to create a flaky crust). Bake the turnovers for 15 to 20 minutes, or until lightly browned.

HAREESH
(MIDDLE EASTERN COCONUT SEMOLINA CAKE)

I love Middle Eastern sweets redolent of cardamom and rosewater, since they remind me of celebrations at the homes of my Persian relatives. *Hareesh*, also called *basbousa*, is a dense Arabic cake made from semolina flour that is then doused in sugar syrup and garnished with pistachios. This version adds coconut into the mix. You may wish to use half of the syrup to start, then determine if you want to use the whole batch. Hareesh is perfect with hot black tea.

MAKES 1 CAKE

½ cup (1 stick) unsalted butter, melted

2 cups heavy cream

⅓ cup milk

⅓ cup plain Greek yogurt

1 teaspoon vanilla extract

2½ cups semolina flour, or more as needed

1 cup grated fresh or frozen coconut

½ cup sugar

½ teaspoon baking powder

¼ teaspoon ground cardamom

Zest of 1 lemon, grated

Chopped pistachios for garnish

syrup

2 cups sugar

1 cup water

1 teaspoon rosewater

1 teaspoon lemon juice

1. Preheat the oven to 350°F (180°C). Grease an 8-inch round cake pan.

2. Combine the butter, cream, milk, yogurt, and vanilla in a large bowl and whisk well until smooth.

3. Whisk together the semolina flour, coconut, sugar, baking powder, cardamom, and lemon zest in a medium bowl. Add to the milk mixture and whisk well until you have a very thick, smooth batter that can be cut with a knife. Add more semolina, a spoonful at a time, if needed.

4. Pour the batter into the prepared pan. Dip a sharp paring knife in hot water and use it to cut a pattern of squares or diamonds that are about 1½ by 1½ inches (see photo) in the batter. Bake the hareesh for 30 to 40 minutes, or until it is firm to the touch and golden brown, and a cake tester inserted into the center comes out clean. If the hareesh isn't browned but is cooked through, you can place it under the broiler for 30 seconds to 1 minute. Cool for 10 minutes, then run your knife along the score lines.

5. While the hareesh is baking, prepare the syrup: Combine the sugar and water in a medium saucepan and bring to a boil over high heat. Reduce the heat to medium and simmer until the mixture becomes a syrup about the consistency of maple syrup, 8 to 10 minutes. Remove from the heat, stir in the rosewater and lemon juice, and allow to cool completely.

6. Pour the syrup over the hot hareesh. Decorate each square of hareesh with the crushed pistachios and allow to cool before serving.

CHINESE-STYLE
SPONGE ROLL
WITH COCONUT CREAM

This recipe is the result of a childhood addiction to the spongy, airy cake that I buy in New York's Chinatown. Think of it as a classic jelly roll with coconut buttercream instead of jelly inside and a much lighter cake. This cake is a bit dangerous, though: because it's so light, you'll want to eat multiple slices! It is perfect with a cup of green or black tea.   MAKES 1 ROLL

cake

- ½ cup cake flour
- 1 tablespoon cornstarch
- ½ teaspoon baking powder
- 3 eggs, separated
- ⅓ cup granulated sugar
- 2½ tablespoons coconut oil, melted
- 2 tablespoons milk
- ⅓ cup cold coconut milk
- 1 teaspoon coconut extract

filling

- ½ cup (1 stick) unsalted butter, slightly softened
- 1½ cups confectioners' sugar
- ¼ teaspoon vanilla extract
- ½ cup coconut cream, chilled

glaze and topping

- 2 tablespoons granulated sugar
- 2 tablespoons water
- Dried sweetened finely grated coconut

1. Preheat the oven to 350°F (180°C). Line a 9- by 13-inch jelly-roll pan with parchment paper.

2. To make the cake, sift the flour, cornstarch, and baking powder together three times in a large bowl to ensure that there are absolutely no lumps. Set aside.

3. Whisk the egg yolks together with half of the granulated sugar in another large bowl and whisk well until the mixture is thickened and doubled in volume, 3 to 4 minutes. Add the coconut oil, milk, and coconut milk, and stir until combined.

4. Add the flour mixture to the egg yolk mixture and mix well so there are no lumps.

5. Combine the egg whites and the remaining sugar in a separate large bowl or the bowl of a stand mixer fitted with a balloon whisk attachment. Using a handheld or stand mixer, whip until stiff peaks form. Fold the egg whites carefully into the batter until thoroughly combined.

6. Pour the batter into the prepared pan. Shake the pan so the batter is even.

7. Fill a second jelly-roll pan with water. Place the cake on the middle rack of the oven and place the water-filled pan on the rack below. Bake the cake for 12 to 15 minutes, or until it is risen and firm and springs back lightly when touched. Remove from the oven and let cool completely.

8. To make the filling, combine the butter, confectioners' sugar, and vanilla in a large bowl or the bowl of a stand mixer fitted with a paddle attachment. Using a handheld or stand mixer, whip at medium speed until light and fluffy, about 1 minute. Add the coconut cream and whip for 1 to 2 minutes longer. Set in the refrigerator until well chilled.

9. To make the glaze, boil the granulated sugar and water together in a small saucepan until reduced and thickened to a syrup, 1 minute. Set aside.

10. Unmold the sponge cake onto a clean piece of parchment paper. Spread the chilled coconut buttercream evenly on top. Carefully begin rolling the cake forward, from the short side, gently pulling the cake into a tight tube as you roll it. When you are done rolling, place the cake seam side down on a platter.

11. Brush the cake with the glaze and then dust with the coconut. Refrigerate for 1 hour.

12. To serve, trim a little off each end of the cake so the first slices are neat. Slice the cake into 1-inch-wide slices and serve.

SALARA
(GUYANESE DANISH)

Salara is a coconut "jelly roll" that is found in every Guyanese bakery or take-out restaurant. The coconut center is most often dyed red using food coloring, which I do not do, but you certainly may. Mixed essence can be found in Caribbean markets or online.   MAKES 1 ROLL

dough

- 1½ teaspoons active dry yeast
- ¼ cup warm water (110°F/45°C)
- ¼ cup plus 1 teaspoon granulated sugar
- ⅔ cup milk
- 1½ tablespoons vegetable shortening
- 1 teaspoon vanilla extract
- 2¼ cups all-purpose flour, or more as needed
- 1 tablespoon butter, melted

filling

- 2½ cups grated fresh coconut
- ½ cup superfine sugar
- ½ teaspoon mixed essence
- ¼ teaspoon ground allspice
- ¼ teaspoon ground cinnamon

1. To make the dough, combine the yeast, warm water, and 1 teaspoon of the granulated sugar in a large bowl or the bowl of a stand mixer, stir, and let sit until frothy and bubbly, about 5 minutes.

2. Meanwhile, heat the milk, vegetable shortening, and the remaining ¼ cup granulated sugar in a small saucepan over medium heat until it just comes to a simmer, the shortening melts, and the sugar is dissolved, 1 to 2 minutes. Stir in the vanilla and set aside to cool to 110°F (45°C).

3. Add the milk mixture to the yeast mixture and mix with a handheld or stand mixer fitted with a paddle attachment. With the mixer going at medium-low speed, slowly add the flour. Then increase the speed to medium and knead the dough until it is smooth and elastic, 3 to 4 minutes. Lightly grease a large bowl with coconut oil. Place the dough in the bowl and cover with plastic wrap. Set in a warm place to rise until doubled in size, about 1 hour.

4. To make the filling, combine the coconut, superfine sugar, mixed essence, allspice, and cinnamon in a large bowl and set aside.

5. Punch down the risen dough and flour a work surface liberally. Roll out the dough into a 10- by 14-inch rectangle. Brush the dough with the melted butter. Spread the filling evenly on top of the rectangle, leaving a 1-inch border of dough on all sides. Roll up the dough from the long side, pulling the dough slightly toward you as you roll.

6. Line a baking sheet with parchment paper. Place the salara roll on the baking sheet, seam side down, and press down on it slightly to flatten it into more of an oval shape. Set the roll aside to rise for 40 minutes.

7. Preheat the oven to 375°F (190°C).

8. Bake for 25 to 30 minutes, or until deeply golden brown. Cool completely, slice, and serve.

guyanese cuisine

Guyana is known for its pastries, which were brought to the country by Dutch colonials in the eighteenth century. Guyanese culture is considered West Indian, even though Guyana is not a Caribbean island. Many of the dishes there are similar to what you might find in Trinidad, thanks to the similar mix of peoples — Africans, East Indians, Chinese, and Europeans.

CLASSIC
COCONUT
CAKE

This cake, beloved of the South, was for many years one of the few ways in which Americans encountered coconut. Even though we've graduated into a whole world of coconut flavor, there is something sublime about this cake. It begins with a simple yellow cake recipe to which coconut extract is added. The frosting is a coconut buttercream that is finished with a flurry of sweetened coconut flakes. MAKES ONE 9-INCH LAYER CAKE

cake

- 1 cup (2 sticks) unsalted butter, softened
- 2 cups granulated sugar
- 5 eggs
- 2½ cups cake flour
- 1 teaspoon baking soda
- 1 teaspoon baking powder
- 1 teaspoon salt
- 1 cup buttermilk
- 1 teaspoon coconut extract
- 1 teaspoon vanilla extract

frosting

- 3 cups confectioners' sugar
- 1 cup (2 sticks) unsalted butter, softened
- 1 cup coconut cream
- 7 tablespoons milk
- 1 teaspoon vanilla extract
- 2 cups sweetened coconut flakes

1. Preheat the oven to 350°F (180°C). Spray two 9- by 2-inch round cake pans with cooking spray.

2. To make the cake, combine the butter and granulated sugar in a large bowl or the bowl of a stand mixer fitted with a paddle attachment. Cream with a handheld or stand mixer at medium speed until light and fluffy, 4 to 5 minutes.

3. Add the eggs one at a time, mixing well after each addition.

4. Sift together the flour, baking soda, baking powder, and salt in a large bowl.

5. Add one-third of the flour mixture to the butter mixture and mix until just combined. Add one-third of the buttermilk and mix until just combined. Repeat, alternating the flour and buttermilk in thirds, until totally combined. Stir in the coconut extract and vanilla.

6. Divide the batter equally between the prepared pans. Bake for
30 to 40 minutes, or until the cakes are golden brown and a cake tester inserted in the center comes out clean. Remove the cakes from the oven and place on a wire rack. Cool in the pans for 10 minutes, then turn the cakes out onto the rack to cool completely.

7. While the cakes are cooling, make the frosting: Combine the confectioners' sugar, butter, coconut cream, milk, and vanilla in a large bowl or the bowl of a stand mixer fitted with a paddle attachment. Cream with a handheld or stand mixer at medium speed until light and fluffy, 4 to 5 minutes. Set aside.

8. When the cakes are cool, place one cake right side up on a cake stand. If the top is too puffy, use a serrated knife to trim and flatten the top. Spread about one-third of the frosting on the top of the cake, then place the second cake upside down on top of the first.

9. Frost the top and sides of the cake with the remaining butter-cream frosting. Press the coconut flakes into the top and sides. Chill in the refrigerator for 30 minutes to set the frosting before serving.

COCONUT LAYER POUND CAKE
WITH LIME CREAM CHEESE FROSTING

Here is another version of the quintessential cake of the American South — the coconut layer cake. This confection ranks alongside red velvet cake and devil's food cake in American culture. In this version, I use coconut pound cake because it's so moist, and because it's denser than traditional yellow cakes, it stands up well to the avalanche of coconut cream cheese frosting and sweetened shredded coconut. The lime zest adds a subtle zing to the topping. MAKES 1 CAKE

cake

- 3 cups cake flour
- ¼ teaspoon coarse salt
- 1 teaspoon baking powder
- 1 cup (2 sticks) unsalted butter, at room temperature
- ¾ cup sour cream
- 2½ cups granulated sugar
- 5 eggs
- ½ teaspoon coconut extract
- ½ teaspoon vanilla extract
- 3 tablespoons coconut milk
- ¾ cup dried unsweetened shredded coconut

frosting

- 2 (8-ounce) packages cream cheese
- 1 cup (2 sticks) unsalted butter, at room temperature
- 8 cups confectioners' sugar
- 4 tablespoons coconut milk
- 2 teaspoons vanilla extract
- 4 tablespoons grated lime zest
- 2 cups sweetened coconut flakes

recipe continues on the next page

COCONUT LAYER POUND CAKE *continued*

1. Preheat the oven to 325°F (165°C). Spray three 9- by 1-inch round cake pans with cooking spray.

2. To make the cake, whisk together the flour, salt, and baking powder in a large bowl. Set aside.

3. Combine the butter, sour cream, and granulated sugar in a large bowl or the bowl of a stand mixer fitted with a paddle attachment. Beat with a handheld or stand mixer until light and fluffy, 5 to 6 minutes. Add the eggs one at a time, beating well after each addition.

4. Add the coconut extract and vanilla to the butter mixture. Reduce the mixer speed to low, add half the flour mixture, then the coconut milk, then the remaining flour mixture. Beat after each addition until just incorporated, stopping the mixer occasionally to scrape down the sides of the bowl. Stir in the shredded coconut.

5. Divide the batter evenly among the prepared cake pans. Bake for 45 minutes, or until a cake tester inserted into the center comes out clean. Let the cakes cool in the pans on a wire rack for 10 minutes. Then set the rack over a sheet of waxed paper, invert the cakes onto the rack, and let cool completely.

6. Make the frosting while the cakes are cooling: Combine the cream cheese and butter in a large bowl or the bowl of a stand mixer fitted with a paddle attachment. Beat with a handheld or stand mixer until light and fluffy, 1 to 2 minutes. Add 2 cups of the confectioners' sugar, then 1 tablespoon of the coconut milk. Repeat, alternating the sugar and coconut milk, beating after each addition. Add the vanilla and lime zest and mix until fully incorporated. Cover the bowl with plastic wrap, placing the wrap right against the frosting, and chill until the cakes are completely cool.

7. Place one of the cakes on a clean work surface and frost it. This is the bottom layer. Place the next layer on top and frost the top and sides. Place the final layer on top. Frost the exterior of the cake with the remaining frosting. Generously sprinkle the top and sides with the coconut flakes, using a flat rubber spatula to press the coconut into the sides of the cake if necessary.

EMILY DICKINSON'S COCONUT CAKE

A little-known fact about the reclusive poet Emily Dickinson is that she was an avid cook and baker. This recipe for "cocoanut" cake (Dickinson's original spelling) was found among her papers. My version makes a fluffier cake than the original, which contained only ½ teaspoon of baking soda. I have upped the baking soda to 1 teaspoon and added 1 tablespoon of baking powder. Top with sugared flowers, which were very popular during Dickinson's time. MAKES 1 CAKE

sugared flowers

- 1 pasteurized egg white or 2 teaspoons powdered egg whites
- 1 teaspoon or 2 tablespoons water
- 10–12 violets, pansies, nasturtiums, or other edible flowers, stems trimmed to ¼ inch (see note)
- ½ cup superfine sugar

cake

- 1 stick unsalted butter, softened
- 1 cup sugar
- 2 eggs
- 1 cup finely grated fresh or frozen coconut
- 2 cups cake flour
- 1 teaspoon baking soda
- 1 tablespoon baking powder
- 1 teaspoon cream of tartar
- ½ cup milk

  Meyer Lemon Glaze (page 154) or Lime Cream Cheese Frosting from Coconut Layer Pound Cake with Lime Cream Cheese Frosting (page 211)

NOTE: *To make the sugared flowers, it's imperative that you start with edible flowers that have not been sprayed with pesticides or fertilizers. The flowers will not keep well, so I suggest making only what's necessary for this cake.*

recipe continues on the next page

EMILY DICKINSON'S COCONUT CAKE *continued*

make the sugared flowers

1. If using powdered egg whites, whisk with 2 tablespoons of water in a small bowl. If using fresh egg white, whisk with 1 teaspoon of water in a small bowl.

2. Using a small, clean paintbrush, brush each flower with egg white. It's helpful to hold the stems with small tweezers while doing this.

3. Dust each painted flower with enough of the superfine sugar to evenly coat. Place on a piece of parchment paper to dry at room temperature for 6 to 8 hours or overnight.

make the cake

4. Preheat the oven to 325°F (165°C). Lightly grease an 8-inch round cake pan or an 8- by 4-inch loaf pan.

5. Combine the butter and sugar in a large bowl or the bowl of a stand mixer fitted with a paddle attachment. Cream with a handheld or stand mixer at medium speed until the butter and sugar are well incorporated, then increase the speed to medium-high and beat until fluffy, about 4 minutes.

6. Lower the mixer speed to medium and add the eggs, one at time, beating well after each addition.

7. Whisk together the coconut, cake flour, baking soda, baking powder, and cream of tartar in a large bowl.

8. With the mixer running at medium-low speed, add one-third of the flour mixture to the butter mixture and blend well. Then add one-third of the milk and mix. Repeat, alternating the flour and milk, until all are used.

9. Pour the batter into the prepared pan. Bake for 45 to 50 minutes, or until a cake tester inserted into the center comes out clean. Let cool in the pan on a wire rack for 10 minutes, then gently turn out of the pan to cool completely.

assemble the cake

10. Glaze the cooled cake with Meyer Lemon Glaze or Lime Cream Cheese Frosting. Decorate with the sugared flowers.

coconut in the U.S.

Emily Dickinson's recipe, which dates to sometime in the mid-nineteenth century, speaks to the fact that coconut has been liked and used in the United States for a long period of time. Whole coconuts were even shipped to New England and the American South during the eighteenth century.

COCONUT BARS

I got the idea for these bars after seeing how many lemon bars were offered at a bake sale at my daughter's school. I realized that the combination of a soft, custardy topping on a firm yet pliable base was incredibly appealing. Instead of a cookie base, these bars have a walnut crust based on the recipe for a crusted flourless chocolate cake that I had more than 20 years ago in San Francisco. MAKES 16 BARS

crust

- ½ cup coconut flour
- 1 cup chopped walnuts
- ¾ cup firmly packed light brown sugar
- 3 tablespoons cold unsalted butter, cut into pieces
- ½ teaspoon salt
- 1 egg

topping

- 4 egg yolks
- ½ cup coconut cream
- ¾ cup granulated sugar
- 1½ cups sweetened coconut flakes
- 1 teaspoon cornstarch
- 1 teaspoon vanilla extract
- 4 ounces melted bittersweet chocolate for drizzling (optional)
- ⅓ cup confectioners' sugar (optional)

1. Preheat the oven to 350°F (180°C). Spray an 8-inch square baking pan with cooking spray.

2. To make the crust, combine the coconut flour and walnuts in a food processor and process into a fine powder.

3. Add the brown sugar, butter, and salt, and process until the mixture clumps together in pea-size grains, about 2 minutes. Add the egg and pulse a few more times until it all comes together in a ball.

4. Remove the dough ball and wrap in plastic wrap. Chill for 20 minutes, then press into the bottom of the prepared pan. Bake the crust for 15 to 20 minutes, or until it is firm and golden brown at the edges.

5. While the crust is baking, make the topping: Combine the egg yolks, coconut cream, and granulated sugar in a large bowl and beat together. Stir in the coconut flakes, cornstarch, and vanilla, and mix well. Pour this mixture over the walnut crust. Bake for 20 to 25 minutes, or until the topping is set and doesn't jiggle when shaken. Remove from the oven and allow to cool completely, then refrigerate for 1 hour.

6. Chop the chocolate, if using, into small pieces and place in a small glass bowl. Microwave for 30 seconds at a time until the chocolate just melts. Stir well and drizzle diagonally over the bars. Let the chocolate set until firm, about 15 minutes, then slice the bars into 2-inch squares. Alternatively, simply dust the bars with confectioners' sugar. Store in an airtight container for up to 3 days.

COCONUT CHEESECAKE
WITH GUAVA GLAZE

Here, I've simply adapted a fail-proof cheesecake recipe that I've used for years. It's a favorite because the texture and taste are classic New York cheesecake through and through — dense and creamy. The best thing about this recipe is that it is extremely easy to prepare: you just place all the ingredients in a food processor and pulse until smooth before pouring into a prepared piecrust. Guava jam is available in Latino markets. MAKES ONE 9-INCH CHEESECAKE

crust

1½ cups graham cracker crumbs

2 tablespoons dried unsweetened finely grated coconut

¼ cup sugar

5½ tablespoons unsalted butter, melted

cheesecake

12 ounces cream cheese, softened

⅓ cup sour cream

⅓ cup coconut cream

½ cup sugar

2 eggs

2 teaspoons coconut extract

2 teaspoons vanilla extract

1 cup guava jam

2 tablespoons coconut sugar

¼ cup dark rum

½ cup dried sweetened shredded coconut

1. Preheat the oven to 325°F (165°C). Lightly spray a 9-inch pie plate with cooking spray.

2. To make the crust, combine the graham cracker crumbs, dried coconut, sugar, and butter in a medium bowl. Stir well; the mixture should have the consistency of wet sand. Press the crumbs into the prepared dish. Bake for 10 minutes. Remove from the oven and allow to cool completely.

3. To make the filling, combine the cream cheese, sour cream, coconut cream, sugar, eggs, coconut extract, and vanilla in a food processor. Pulse until thick and smooth, without lumps, about 1 minute. Do not overprocess or the mixture will become runny.

4. Pour the cream cheese mixture on top of the crust. Bake for 50 minutes, or until the top of the cheesecake doesn't jiggle when shaken.

5. While the cheesecake is baking, combine the guava jam, coconut sugar, and rum in a small saucepan over low heat. Simmer, whisking, until the mixture is thickened, 10 to 15 minutes. Set aside to cool.

6. Slide the pie plate out of the oven, pour the guava mixture on the middle of the cheesecake, and smooth it evenly over the surface with the back of a spoon. Spread the coconut evenly on top. Turn the oven off and slide the cheesecake back inside. Allow the cheesecake to sit in the oven until the oven completely cools down.

7. Refrigerate the cheesecake for at least 8 hours and up to overnight. Serve chilled.

COCONUT
CREAM PIE

I like both coconut cream pie and coconut custard pie, but if pressed, I'd have to say this cream pie is my favorite pie of all time. The lightened coconut custard is delicious without being heavy or too sweet, which makes it an ideal dessert for a summer picnic, a holiday meal, or anything in between. If you can't find sweetened finely shredded coconut, place regular sweetened shredded coconut in a food processor and pulse until fine.   MAKES ONE 9-INCH PIE

crust

1⅓   cups all-purpose flour

1   teaspoon salt

½   cup (1 stick) unsalted butter, cut into small cubes

3   tablespoons ice water, or more as needed

coconut custard

2   tablespoons water

1   tablespoon cornstarch

1¼   cups coconut milk

½   cup sugar

⅛   teaspoon salt

4   egg yolks

1   teaspoon coconut extract

1   teaspoon vanilla extract

¾   cup dried sweetened finely shredded coconut

filling and topping

2   cups heavy cream

½   cup sugar

1   teaspoon coconut extract

1   teaspoon vanilla extract

⅓   cup toasted coconut flakes for garnish

1. To make the crust, combine the flour and salt in a food processor and process briefly to mix. Add the butter and pulse until the mixture forms pea-size chunks.

2. Pour the crust mixture into a large bowl and gradually add the ice water, mixing gently until the mixture just comes together into a ball. Wrap the dough in plastic wrap and chill in the refrigerator for 1 hour. You can also flatten the dough ball into a disk, wrap well, and freeze for up to 1 month.

3. Preheat the oven to 350°F (180°C).

4. Liberally flour a work surface and flatten the chilled dough ball on it. Flour your rolling pin and roll the dough out into a disk 10 to 11 inches wide.

5. Line a 9-inch pie plate with the piecrust and fold the edges under. Crimp them to make a decorative pattern. Using a fork, prick the crust all over, then cover with a piece of parchment paper or aluminum foil and add pie weights. Bake the crust for 20 minutes. Remove the pie weights and parchment and bake for 5 to 10 minutes longer, or until the crust is lightly browned. Remove from the oven and set aside to cool completely.

6. To make the coconut custard, whisk together the water and cornstarch in a small bowl. Set aside.

7. Combine the coconut milk, the sugar, and the salt in a medium saucepan. Heat over medium-low heat, whisking frequently to melt the sugar, until the liquid just starts to simmer around the edges of the pan, 3 to 4 minutes.

8. Place the egg yolks in a large bowl and beat to break them up. Slowly drizzle the hot coconut milk mixture into the eggs, whisking the whole time. When all of the hot milk mixture has been added to the egg yolks, return the mixture to the saucepan.

9. Reduce the heat to low and whisk in the cornstarch slurry. Cook, whisking constantly, until the mixture starts to thicken up like pudding, 4 to 5 minutes.

10. Mix in the coconut extract, vanilla, and shredded coconut. Cook for 1 minute, then remove from the heat and chill until completely cold, about 1 hour.

11. To make the filling and topping, combine the heavy cream, sugar, coconut extract, and vanilla in a large bowl or the bowl of a stand mixer fitted with a balloon whisk attachment. Whip the cream with a handheld or stand mixer at medium-high speed until stiff peaks form, 2 to 3 minutes.

12. Gently fold one-quarter of the whipped cream into the coconut custard. Pour this mixture into the prepared piecrust and smooth the top, then chill until firm, 1 to 2 hours. Spoon the rest of the whipped cream on top of the filled pie. Make sure the surface is totally covered. Garnish with the toasted coconut and chill in the refrigerator for 4 to 6 hours. Serve chilled.

COCONUT CREAM AND CHOCOLATE CREAM LAYER PIE

There are chocolate cream pie aficionados like my husband, and then there are coconut cream pie aficionados like me. I came up with this pie to meld the best of both worlds. Each slice has layers of chocolate and coconut for a lovely presentation. We often serve this at Thanksgiving for something a little different from the standard pumpkin, sweet potato, or pecan offerings. **MAKES ONE 10-INCH PIE**

crust

- 1⅓ cups all-purpose flour, or more as needed
- 1 teaspoon salt
- ½ cup (1 stick) unsalted butter, cut into small cubes
- 3 tablespoons ice water, or more as needed

chocolate cream filling

- 2 tablespoons water
- 1 tablespoon cornstarch
- ½ cup milk
- ¾ cup heavy cream
- ⅓ cup sugar
- ⅛ teaspoon salt
- 3 egg yolks
- 4 ounces bittersweet chocolate
- 1 teaspoon unsweetened cocoa powder
- 1 teaspoon vanilla extract
- 2 tablespoons cold unsalted butter, sliced

coconut cream filling

- 2 tablespoons water
- ½ tablespoon cornstarch
- ½ cup coconut milk
- ¼ cup sugar
- ⅛ teaspoon salt
- 2 egg yolks
- ½ teaspoon coconut extract
- ½ teaspoon vanilla extract
- ⅔ cup dried sweetened finely shredded coconut
- ½ cup heavy cream
- 2 tablespoons sugar

topping

- ½ cup heavy cream
- 2 tablespoons sugar
- ½ teaspoon coconut extract
- ½ teaspoon vanilla extract
- ½ cup toasted coconut flakes
  Shaved bittersweet chocolate for garnish

recipe continues on the next page

COCONUT CREAM AND CHOCOLATE CREAM LAYER PIE

continued

make the piecrust

1. Combine the flour and salt in a food processor and process briefly to mix. Add the butter and pulse until you have chunks about the size of peas.

2. Pour the crust mixture into a large bowl and gradually add the ice water, mixing gently until the mixture just comes together into a ball. Wrap the dough in plastic wrap and refrigerate for 1 hour before using. You can also flatten the dough ball into a disk, wrap well, and freeze for up to 1 month.

3. Preheat the oven to 350°F (180°C).

4. Liberally flour a work surface and flatten the chilled dough ball on it. Flour your rolling pin and roll the dough out into a disk about 12 to 13 inches wide.

5. Line a 10-inch deep-dish pie plate with the piecrust and fold the edges under. Crimp them to make a decorative pattern. Use a fork to prick the crust all over, then cover with a piece of parchment paper or aluminum foil and add pie weights. Bake the crust for 20 minutes. Remove the pie weights and parchment and bake for 5 to 10 minutes longer, or until the crust is lightly browned. Remove from the oven and set aside to cool.

make the chocolate cream filling

6. Whisk together the water and the cornstarch in a small bowl. Set aside.

7. Combine the milk, heavy cream, sugar, and salt in a medium saucepan. Heat over medium-low heat, whisking frequently to melt the sugar, until it just starts to simmer around the edges of the pan, 3 to 4 minutes.

8. Place the egg yolks in a large bowl and beat to break them up. Slowly drizzle the hot milk mixture into the eggs, whisking vigorously the whole time. When all of the hot milk mixture has been added to the egg yolks, return the mixture to the saucepan.

9. Reduce the heat to low and add the cornstarch slurry. Cook, whisking constantly, until the mixture starts to thicken up like pudding, 4 to 5 minutes.

10. Remove the custard from the heat and add the bittersweet chocolate and cocoa powder, whisking until all of the chocolate is melted and well mixed. Whisk in the vanilla and then add the butter, whisking until it is melted and fully incorporated. Place plastic wrap over the chocolate cream, laying the wrap right against the custard, and chill in the refrigerator until completely cold, about 2 hours.

make the coconut cream filling

11. Whisk together the water and the cornstarch in a small bowl. Set aside.

12. Combine the coconut milk, sugar, and salt in a medium saucepan. Heat over medium-low heat, whisking frequently to melt the sugar, until the liquid just starts to simmer around the edges of the pan, 3 to 4 minutes.

13. Place the egg yolks in a large bowl and beat to break them up. Slowly drizzle the hot coconut milk mixture into the eggs, whisking the whole time. When all of the hot milk mixture has been added to the egg yolks, return the mixture to the saucepan.

14. Reduce the heat to low and whisk in the cornstarch slurry. Cook, whisking constantly, until the mixture starts to thicken up like pudding, 4 to 5 minutes.

15. Mix in the coconut extract, vanilla, and shredded coconut. Cook for 1 minute longer, then remove from the heat.

16. Combine the heavy cream and sugar in a large bowl or the bowl of a stand mixer fitted with a balloon whisk attachment. Whip with a hand-held or stand mixer at medium-high speed until stiff peaks form, 2 to 3 minutes. Gently fold the whipped cream into the coconut custard. Refrigerate the custard mixture until completely cold, about 1 hour.

assemble the pie

17. Spoon half of the coconut custard into the pie shell. Top with an equal amount of chocolate custard. Layer the remaining coconut custard on top, and then layer the remaining chocolate custard on top of that. The top layer may be higher than the level of the pie plate rim, but that's okay. Chill in the refrigerator for 1 hour.

18. When the pie is completely chilled, make the whipped cream topping: Combine the heavy cream, sugar, coconut extract, and vanilla in a large bowl or the bowl of a stand mixer fitted with a balloon whisk attachment. Whip with a handheld or stand mixer at medium-high speed until stiff peaks form, 2 to 3 minutes.

19. Spoon the whipped cream on top of the pie, smoothing lightly so that it covers the surface of the pie in soft peaks. Garnish with the toasted coconut and shaved chocolate. Keep refrigerated and serve cold.

COCONUT CUSTARD PIE

In my young life, there were a few bastions of commercial coconut goodness. There was the single coconut Life Saver in the tropical fruit–flavored roll of that candy, the Mounds candy bar, and, finally, the coconut custard pie made by Entenmann's, the beloved New York–based commercial bakery. This is my homage to that pie. MAKES ONE 9-INCH PIE

crust

- 1⅓ cups all-purpose flour, or more as needed
- 1 teaspoon salt
- ½ cup (1 stick) unsalted butter, cut into small cubes
- 3 tablespoons ice water, or more as needed

filling

- 4 eggs
- ¾ cup sugar
- 2 tablespoons coconut flour
- 2 tablespoons cornstarch
- ¾ cup dried unsweetened finely grated coconut
- 1 cup coconut cream
- 1 teaspoon coconut extract
- 1 teaspoon vanilla extract
- ⅛ teaspoon ground nutmeg
- ⅛ teaspoon salt
  Whipped cream for garnish (optional)

1. To make the piecrust, combine the flour and salt in a food processor and process briefly to mix. Add the butter and pulse until you have chunks about the size of peas.

2. Pour the crust mixture into a large bowl and gradually add the ice water, mixing gently until the mixture just comes together into a ball. Wrap the dough in plastic wrap and chill in the refrigerator for 1 hour before using. You can also flatten the dough ball into a disk, wrap well, and freeze for up to 1 month.

3. Preheat the oven to 325°F (165°C).

4. Liberally flour a work surface and flatten the chilled dough ball on it. Flour your rolling pin and roll the dough out into a disk about 10 to 11 inches wide.

5. Line a 9-inch pie plate with the piecrust and fold the edges under. Crimp them to make a decorative pattern.

6. To make the filling, combine the eggs and sugar in a large bowl or the bowl of a stand mixer fitted with a paddle attachment. With a handheld or stand mixer, beat for 3 minutes. Add the coconut flour and cornstarch and mix at medium-high speed for 2 minutes.

7. Add the coconut and stir well to combine. Add the coconut cream, coconut extract, vanilla, nutmeg, and salt, stirring well to thoroughly combine. Pour this mixture into the prepared piecrust.

8. Bake for 30 to 40 minutes, or until the filling is set and does not jiggle when shaken. Don't overbake.

9. Remove the pie from the oven and allow to cool completely, then refrigerate for at least 1 hour before serving. Serve with fresh whipped cream, if desired.

COCONUT LEMONGRASS
SEMIFREDDO

Semifreddo is an excellent option for those who love frozen desserts but may not necessarily want to go to the trouble of churning ice cream. *Semifreddo* means "semifrozen" in Italian, and this Italian classic features whipped cream that is folded into custard. I've flavored the coconut milk with lemon zest and lemongrass before whisking it into egg yolks for a custard. Mixed raspberries and blackberries are a gorgeous accompaniment to this dish. MAKES 1 LOAF

¾ cup sliced almonds

½ cup dried sweetened shredded coconut

2 tablespoons water

1 tablespoon cornstarch

2 cups coconut milk

1¼ cups sugar

1 stalk fresh lemongrass, sliced in half and bruised well

2 teaspoons grated lemon zest

2 egg yolks

1 cup heavy cream

1 cup mixed raspberries and blackberries

1. Line an 8- by 4-inch loaf pan with two large pieces of overlapping plastic wrap and let them hang over the long sides of the pan. Layer the almonds and the coconut on the bottom.

2. Whisk together the water and the cornstarch in a small bowl. Set aside.

3. Combine the coconut milk, 1 cup of the sugar, lemongrass, and the lemon zest in a medium saucepan over medium heat. Bring to a low simmer, stirring often, until all the sugar melts, 3 to 4 minutes. Cover the pan and remove from the heat. Set aside for about 1 hour so the lemongrass stalk can steep and release its flavor.

4. Put the saucepan back over medium heat and bring just to a simmer. Strain the mixture into another pan or a heatproof pitcher.

5. Whisk the egg yolks together in a wide deep bowl. Slowly add the coconut milk mixture in a thin, slow stream, whisking constantly to incorporate fully. Return the mixture to the saucepan over low heat. Add the cornstarch mixture and whisk constantly until the mixture thickens, 3 to 4 minutes. Remove from the heat and refrigerate for 1 hour.

recipe continues on the next page

COCONUT
LEMONGRASS
SEMIFREDDO

continued

6. Pour the custard into a large bowl or the bowl of a stand mixer with a whisk attachment. With a handheld or stand mixer, whip at medium-high speed until the custard is thickened, 4 to 5 minutes.

7. Pour the heavy cream into another large bowl and whip with a handheld mixer until stiff peaks form, 1 to 2 minutes. Fold it gently into the custard.

8. Spoon the custard cream into the prepared loaf pan and smooth. Tap the pan on the counter to remove air bubbles. Fold the plastic wrap over the top of the custard and freeze until firm, about 6 hours or up to overnight. As long as it's well wrapped, you can leave the semifreddo in the freezer for up to 3 days before unmolding.

9. Gently mix together the berries and the remaining ¼ cup sugar in a medium bowl.

10. Unwrap the semifreddo and place a platter over the loaf pan. Turn the loaf pan over onto the platter and unmold the semi-freddo. Gently pull away the plastic wrap. Some of the almonds and coconut may pull away with the wrap; just press them gently back into place.

11. Arrange the berries on top of the semifreddo. Slice to serve.

VEGAN COCONUT
ICE CREAM

This ice cream recipe is a go-to in my family. I started making it in the days when it was virtually impossible to get any kind of coconut product in America except for, maybe, a Mounds bar or an occasional coconut-crusted vanilla bar from some select ice cream trucks. Because I was interested in coconut flavor above all, I created this recipe using only coconut milk and coconut cream. MAKES 1 QUART

1½ cups coconut milk

½ cup coconut cream

¾ cup sugar

1 tablespoon agar powder

1 teaspoon coconut extract

1 teaspoon vanilla extract

1 cup sweetened coconut flakes

1. Combine the coconut milk, coconut cream, sugar, and agar in a medium saucepan over medium-low heat. Bring to a simmer, stirring constantly until the sugar is dissolved.

2. Remove the pan from the heat and stir in the coconut extract and vanilla. Set aside to cool completely.

3. Place the coconut in a food processor and pulse until it has the texture of coarse sand, 10 to 15 seconds. Stir the coconut into the coconut milk mixture.

4. Churn the coconut mixture in your ice cream maker, following the manufacturer's directions. When firm, place in the freezer in a quart-size container to set completely, about 4 hours.

VARIATION: COCONUT ICE CREAM SANDWICHES

For a wonderful (though not vegan) variation, sandwich some of this ice cream between shortbreads from the Coconut-Caramel-Chocolate Shortbreads recipe (page 192) and pat sweetened coconut flakes around the edges. Freeze these between sheets of waxed paper for a very grown-up version of traditional ice cream sandwiches.

COCONUT-SOURSOP (GUANABANA)
SORBET

This sorbet is one of my absolute favorites. Soursop, which is called *guanabana* in Latin America, is a naturally sweet and tart green fruit with a soft white flesh. You can find frozen soursop purée in Caribbean or Spanish markets but also, increasingly, in the Latino section of your grocer's freezer. This sorbet is a wonderful palate cleanser to serve between courses, as you would a lemon sorbet. MAKES 1 QUART

½ cup sugar

½ cup water

1 cup coconut water

1 cup soursop (guanabana) purée

Zest of 1 lime, grated

1 tablespoon freshly squeezed lime juice

1. Combine the sugar and water in a small saucepan and bring to a simmer over medium heat. Simmer until the mixture is reduced and thickened into a syrup roughly the consistency of honey, 8 to 10 minutes.

2. Combine the coconut water and soursop in a medium saucepan over medium-low heat and bring to just under a simmer. This is to warm the mixture so that the simple syrup doesn't harden when combined. Add the simple syrup, lime zest, and lime juice, and mix well.

3. Allow the mixture to cool, then churn in your ice cream maker to sorbet stage, following the manufacturer's directions. Scoop the sorbet into a quart container and freeze for at least 8 hours or until firm. The sorbet will keep for up to 2 weeks in the freezer.

COCONUT
PANNA COTTA

This light molded pudding is an ideal summer dessert. It's not too sweet, and the consistency is smooth and silky. Sophisticated and delicate, the panna cotta is impressive on the plate, belying how easy it is to make. It's particularly nice garnished with fresh chopped fruit to add tang and color. The panna cotta will need to chill for at least 8 hours before serving, so plan ahead. **MAKES 4 SERVINGS**

⅔ cup sugar

1½ cups coconut milk

½ cup cream of coconut (sweetened coconut cream), such as Coco Lopez brand

2 teaspoons agar powder

1 tablespoon spiced rum

Pineapple, mango, strawberry, or kiwifruit, chopped small, for garnish (optional)

1. Place the sugar in a small saucepan over medium-low heat and cook, stirring with a wooden spoon, until it melts. Continue to cook, swirling the pan, until the melted sugar is deeply golden brown. Divide the melted sugar among four ¾-cup (6-ounce) ramekins, and tilt the ramekins so the sugar coats the bottom. Set aside.

2. Whisk together the coconut milk, cream of coconut, and agar in a medium saucepan over medium-low heat. Bring the mixture to a simmer and whisk well until it is completely incorporated and combined. Simmer gently for 1 minute, then remove the mixture from the heat. Add the rum and mix well.

3. Allow the mixture to cool until it is just warm and then divide evenly among the prepared ramekins. Chill in the refrigerator for at least 8 hours and up to overnight.

4. Pour boiling water into a shallow bowl. To unmold the panna cotta, dip the bottom of a ramekin in the hot water. Do not let any water slosh over into the panna cotta. Run a sharp paring knife around the edges of the panna cotta. Turn a dessert plate upside down on top of the panna cotta and then flip it over. The dessert should come out easily. Repeat with all the panna cotta. Garnish with chopped fruit, if using. When wrapped well in plastic wrap, any leftovers will keep in the refrigerator for up to 4 days.

COCONUT
MACAROONS

GLUTEN-FREE

DAIRY-FREE

Coconut macaroons, mostly known as a popular treat at Passover, are one of the most unsung American desserts. While the preparation is easy, macaroons require constant vigilance during the stovetop stage. Using a double boiler to make the batter is a good way to ensure it doesn't scorch. Dried unsweetened shredded coconut (Bob's Red Mill and King Arthur Flour both make a version specifically for macaroons) is an absolute essential to achieve just the right consistency. MAKES ABOUT 20 COOKIES

4 egg whites, at room temperature

1 cup sugar

¼ teaspoon coarse salt

⅛ teaspoon cream of tartar

1 teaspoon vanilla extract

3 cups dried unsweetened finely grated coconut

1. Preheat the oven to 325°F (165°C). Line a large baking sheet with parchment paper or a silicone mat.

2. Combine the egg whites, sugar, salt, and cream of tartar in a double boiler or a heatproof bowl set over a saucepan of simmering water. Cook over low heat, whisking lightly, until the sugar is dissolved and the mixture is creamy and warm to the touch, 3 to 4 minutes.

3. Add the vanilla and mix well, then add the coconut. Using a wooden spoon, stir constantly until the mixture begins to come away from the sides of the bowl, 8 to 10 minutes.

4. Remove the coconut mixture from the heat. Using a 1-tablespoon ice cream scoop or a tablespoon, drop scoopfuls of the mixture onto the prepared baking sheet.

5. Bake for 20 to 25 minutes, or until light golden brown. Allow to cool completely before serving. Coconut macaroons can be stored in an airtight jar or ziplock bag for up to 1 week.

CHOCOLATE-DIPPED MACAROONS

If you prefer your coconut macaroons dipped in chocolate, melt
8 ounces of semisweet chocolate chips in a medium bowl in the
microwave. Heat them on high in 10-second intervals, stirring
the chocolate between each interval. It should take no more than
50 seconds to melt the chips completely. Alternatively, melt the
chocolate in a double boiler over medium heat, stirring frequently,
until all the chips are melted.

Once your chocolate is melted, carefully dip the flat bottom surface
of each macaroon into the melted chocolate. Allow the excess to
drip off, then place the macaroons on a tray lined with waxed paper
until they are firm. Store in an airtight container.

BIBINGKA
(FILIPINO COCONUT CAKE)

Bibingka is a naturally gluten-free dessert from the Philippines that has a pleasantly silky, pudding-like texture. It is traditionally baked in a clay pot lined with banana leaves and then nestled in hot coals. To approximate that taste in a Western oven, I line each cup of my muffin pan with two pieces of banana leaf (available in Caribbean markets). If you want a more authentic experience, you can slightly char the banana leaves over an open flame before using them to line the muffin cups. MAKES 12 CAKES

1 (16-ounce) package banana leaves (optional)

½ cup sugar

1¾ cups sweet rice flour

1 tablespoon gluten-free baking powder

½ teaspoon salt

1 cup coconut milk

¼ cup (½ stick) unsalted butter, melted and cooled

3 eggs

½ cup sweetened coconut flakes

1. Preheat the oven to 350°F (180°C). If using banana leaves, cut them into 16 strips that are 3 inches by 4 inches. Line each cup of an 8-cup muffin pan with two overlapping strips of banana leaf.

2. Whisk together the sugar, rice flour, baking powder, and salt in a large bowl.

3. Combine the coconut milk, butter, and eggs in another large bowl and beat very well.

4. Add the flour mixture to the milk mixture and, using a whisk, beat the batter well.

5. Evenly divide the batter among the prepared muffin cups, then top the cups evenly with the coconut flakes. Bake for 18 to 20 minutes, or until the bibingka are puffed and the center does not jiggle when shaken. Serve hot.

a filipino christmas tradition

Bibingka is commonly eaten after midnight mass on Christmas Eve in the Philippines. Churches often give away the treat to parishioners after services. A similar cake is also made for Chinese New Year in Malaysia. Made from sweet rice flour and coconut milk, bibingka has many variations. Being a coconut purist, I add only sweetened coconut flakes to my bibingka, but some people add cheddar cheese or a salted duck egg. I've also seen versions with banana or cream cheese. If you choose to add any of these, place about 1 teaspoon of each topping in the muffin pan after you've filled it with bibingka batter.

TEMBLEQUE

Tembleque means "trembling" in Spanish, and it's a good description for this jiggly coconut pudding made with coconut milk, sugar, and cornstarch. Tembleque is very light and incredibly easy to prepare. You can make it more elegant by chilling it in a pretty mold and dusting it with cinnamon or serving it with sliced fruit. MAKES 4–6 SERVINGS

½ cup cornstarch

3½ cups coconut milk

¾ cup sugar

⅛ teaspoon salt

Cinnamon for dusting

Sliced strawberries for garnish

Small fresh mint leaves for garnish

1. Combine the cornstarch and ½ cup of the coconut milk in a small bowl and stir until the cornstarch dissolves. Set aside.

2. Combine the remaining 3 cups coconut milk and the sugar in a medium saucepan over medium heat. Whisk constantly until the sugar is dissolved, 1 to 2 minutes. Stir in the salt, add the cornstarch slurry, and continue whisking until the mixture boils and thickens like a heavy gravy, 5 to 6 minutes.

3. Pour into four ¾-cup (6-ounce) molds and chill in the refrigerator for at least 4 hours and up to 2 days. If you plan to chill the tembleque for a longer period, wrap the molds in plastic wrap.

4. Unmold the tembleque by running a thin, sharp paring knife around the edge of each mold. Place a plate over the top of the mold and turn the mold over onto it. The pudding should come right out. Dust lightly with cinnamon and then garnish with some strawberry slices and mint leaves.

VARIATION: TEMBLEQUE TOPPINGS

Though most often associated with Puerto Rico, tembleque exists in one form or another throughout Latin America, and the flavoring agents change depending on locale. In Brazil, for example, it's called *manjar branco* and is topped with prunes poached in wine. An identical pudding can be found in Hawaii, where it is called *haupia*. In Hong Kong and other parts of China, another similar pudding is cut into squares and called "coconut bar."

COCONUT-RUM
CRÈME
BRÛLÉE

Crème brûlée is a seemingly simple dessert that truly tests the skill of the cook. Not only must you create a creamy custard, but it has to stay nice and cool even after you've "brûléed" or broiled the sugar on top. The secret is to use coconut sugar, which melts quickly and creates a nice hard caramel crust without heating up the custard below. MAKES 4 SERVINGS

2 tablespoons water

1 tablespoon cornstarch

1½ cups heavy cream

½ cup coconut cream

½ vanilla bean

6 egg yolks

½ cup granulated sugar

½ teaspoon coconut extract

1 tablespoon good-quality dark rum

Coconut sugar for topping

Fresh raspberries for serving

1. Whisk together the water and the cornstarch in a small bowl. Set aside.

2. Combine the cream and coconut cream in a medium saucepan over medium heat and whisk well to combine. Split the vanilla bean down the center with a sharp paring knife and scrape out the seeds. Add these to the pan, along with the bean itself.

3. Heat the cream mixture until it just simmers, 1 to 2 minutes. Remove from the heat and allow the mixture to sit for 30 minutes for the vanilla bean to infuse flavor.

4. Preheat the oven to 300°F (150°C).

5. Return the pan to the heat and bring the mixture to a low simmer over medium-low heat. Whisk well. Remove the vanilla bean and discard.

6. In a heatproof bowl, whisk the egg yolks and granulated sugar together, then add the cream mixture in a thin, steady stream, whisking vigorously the whole time.

7. Stir in the coconut extract and rum and divide the mixture evenly among four ¾-cup (6-ounce) ramekins. Place the ramekins in a baking dish that is deep enough to hold them and add enough water to reach halfway up the sides of the ramekins. Cover the whole dish tightly with aluminum foil.

8. Bake the custards for 45 to 50 minutes, or until they are firm around the edges. When you jiggle them, they should not be loose in the middle. Remove the custards and allow them to cool for 10 to 15 minutes, then cover with plastic wrap and refrigerate overnight.

9. To serve the crème brûlée, evenly dust each custard top with a thin layer of the coconut sugar (about 1 teaspoon per custard). Using a kitchen torch, lightly melt the sugar to form a hard caramel top. Alternatively, you may place the custards on a cookie sheet under the broiler and cook until the sugar melts, about 1 minute. Serve with fresh raspberries on the side.

COCONUT RICE PUDDING
WITH PINEAPPLE BRÛLÉE

GLUTEN-FREE

DAIRY-FREE

This rice pudding is simply called "sweet rice" in the Caribbean. The rum gives this soothing dish a sophisticated air, although you can certainly omit it. Raisins are nice touch if you like them, and currants will work, too. The richly caramelized pineapple spears add a sweet-tart element, while the crunch of the coconut chips turns this humble comfort food into something spectacular. MAKES 4 SERVINGS

1 cup long-grain white rice

1½ cup water

2 cups coconut milk

½ cup sugar

Pinch of ground cinnamon

Pinch of ground nutmeg

½ teaspoon dark spiced rum, such as Myers's brand (optional)

¼ teaspoon coconut extract

¼ teaspoon vanilla extract

2 tablespoons raisins (optional)

½ large fresh pineapple, cut into spears about 4 inches long and 1 inch wide

3 tablespoons coconut sugar

2 tablespoons toasted coconut chips

1. To wash the rice, place it in a deep bowl and add enough cold water to cover by 3 inches. Swirl the rice around with your hand until the water becomes cloudy. Carefully drain the water. Repeat this four or five times, or until the water runs clear. Set the rice aside.

2. Bring 1½ cups of water to a boil in a medium saucepan and add the rice. Simmer, uncovered, for 8 to 10 minutes, skimming off any foam from the top of the rice as necessary.

3. Drain the rice and return it to the saucepan with the coconut milk, sugar, cinnamon, and nutmeg. Stir once. Bring to a simmer and cook, uncovered, over medium-low heat for 10 minutes. Add the rum, if using, along with the coconut extract, vanilla, and raisins, if desired, and simmer for 5 minutes longer. Stir occasionally to ensure that the pudding does not scorch on the bottom. The finished pudding should be soft and thick, but not sticky, and have some liquid.

4. While the pudding is cooking, preheat the oven broiler. Spray a baking sheet with cooking spray or line with parchment paper or a silicone mat.

5. Place the pineapple spears on the prepared baking sheet. Spray the spears lightly with cooking spray, then sprinkle evenly with the coconut sugar. Place in the hot oven and cook for 2 to 4 minutes, or until the sugar melts and starts to caramelize. Remove from the oven and allow to cool slightly, 2 to 3 minutes.

6. Divide the rice pudding evenly among four small bowls and garnish with pineapple spears standing up in the pudding. Sprinkle the top of the pudding with the toasted coconut and serve.

COCONUT-CINNAMON ROLLS
WITH TOASTED COCONUT– CREAM CHEESE FROSTING

For this recipe, I've taken a basic sweet roll dough and added coconut. These are a Christmas Day tradition in my house, and we eat them while opening presents. Fluffy and pillowy, they are just sweet enough, and the cream cheese frosting adds a nice balance to the filling. You can let the rolls rise in the refrigerator overnight rather than on a countertop if you want to bake them first thing in the morning. MAKES 12 OVERSIZE ROLLS

rolls

- ¼ cup warm water (110°F/45°C)
- 2¼ teaspoons (1 packet) active dry yeast
- ¼ cup plus 1 teaspoon granulated sugar
- ½ cup (1 stick) unsalted butter, softened
- 2 eggs
- ¾ cup warm milk (110°F/45°C)
- 1 teaspoon salt
- ½ teaspoon vanilla extract
- 2¾–3¼ cups all-purpose flour, or more as needed

filling

- ⅓ cup firmly packed light brown sugar
- ⅓ cup granulated sugar
- 3 tablespoons ground cinnamon
- 2 cups grated fresh or frozen coconut
- ½ cup (1 stick) unsalted butter
- ¼ cup light corn syrup

frosting

- 2 (8-ounce) packages cream cheese, softened
- ⅓ cup coconut cream
- ¾ cup confectioners' sugar
- 1 teaspoon coconut extract
- 1 teaspoon vanilla extract
- Toasted coconut for garnish (optional)

1. To prepare the rolls, place the warm water in a small bowl and sprinkle the yeast over the top. Add 1 teaspoon of the granulated sugar. Stir and set aside in a warm place until the yeast is bubbly and frothy, about 5 minutes.

2. Put the yeast mixture in a large bowl or the bowl of a stand mixer fitted with a paddle attachment. Add the butter and the remaining ¼ cup sugar and mix well with a handheld or stand mixer. You may still have lumps of butter, but that's okay.

3. Add the eggs and mix well. Add the milk, salt, and vanilla, and mix for 1 minute. Add the flour 1 cup at a time, mixing at medium speed, until you get a soft, slightly sticky dough. Add additional flour, if needed, by the tablespoon to achieve this texture. Lightly oil a large bowl with coconut oil. Put the dough in the greased bowl and cover with plastic wrap. Set aside in a warm place to rise until doubled in size, about 1 hour.

4. To make the filling, combine half of the brown and granulated sugars, half of the cinnamon, and the coconut in a medium bowl. Mix well. Set aside.

5. Combine the butter and corn syrup in a small saucepan over medium-low heat. Stir until the butter melts. Remove from the heat.

6. To form the rolls, dust a clean work surface liberally with flour and roll out the dough into a 15- by 13-inch rectangle. Brush half of the corn syrup mixture on the dough, leaving about 1 inch of dough around the edges. Spread the coconut-cinnamon mixture on top, reserving 3 tablespoons for the pan.

7. Roll up the dough, like a jelly roll, from the long side. Gently pull the dough toward you while rolling in order to get a tight roll. Slice the roll crosswise into ½-inch-wide slices.

8. Pour the rest of the corn syrup mixture into a 9- by 13-inch baking dish and sprinkle the remaining coconut-cinnamon mixture on top. Nestle the rolls in the baking dish with about ½ inch of space between them. Cover the rolls loosely with a clean dish towel and set aside to rise in a warm place until doubled in size, about 1 hour.

recipe continues on the next page

COCONUT-CINNAMON ROLLS

continued

9. Preheat the oven to 350°F (180°C).

10. Bake the rolls for 25 to 30 minutes, or until puffed and golden brown on top. Remove and let cool slightly.

11. While the rolls are baking, make the frosting: Combine the cream cheese and coconut cream in a large bowl or the bowl of a stand mixer fitted with the paddle attachment. Mix with a handheld or stand mixer at medium speed until the mixture is fluffy and well combined, 2 to 3 minutes. Add the confectioners' sugar, coconut extract, and vanilla, and mix until combined, 2 to 3 minutes longer.

12. Spread the frosting on the slightly cooled rolls while they are still in the pan. Garnish with the toasted coconut, if using. The rolls may be kept, well wrapped, for up to 2 days at room temperature.

HAWAIIAN MALASADAS WITH HAUPIA (COCONUT PUDDING FILLING)

Malasadas are a Portuguese doughnut traditionally served on Fat Tuesday — Mardi Gras. Today, malasadas are a popular treat in Hawaii, and the fillings include jellies made from local fruits like mango, pineapple, and papaya, as well as *haupia*, a cornstarch-thickened coconut pudding. MAKES 24 DOUGHNUTS

malasadas

- 2¼ teaspoons (1 packet) active dry yeast
- ¼ cup warm water (110°F/45°C)
- ⅓ cup plus 1 teaspoon sugar
- ⅔ cup warm milk (110°F/45°C)
- 1 teaspoon vanilla extract
- 4 eggs
- ½ cup (1 stick) unsalted butter, melted and cooled
- 4 cups all-purpose flour, or more as needed
- ½ teaspoon salt
  Safflower oil for frying

filling

- ¼ cup cornstarch
- 2½ cups coconut milk
- ⅔ cup sugar
- ⅛ teaspoon salt

topping

- ⅓ cup ground cinnamon
- ⅓ cup sugar

1. To prepare the malasadas, combine the yeast and water in a large bowl or the bowl of a stand mixer and add 1 teaspoon of the sugar. Stir and set aside until the yeast is frothy and bubbly, about 5 minutes.

2. Add the milk and vanilla and mix with a handheld or stand mixer at medium speed until totally combined. Add the eggs one at a time, beating well after each addition. Stir in the butter and mix well.

3. Combine the flour, salt, and remaining ⅓ cup sugar in a medium bowl and mix well. Add this to the yeast mixture and mix at medium speed until you have a soft, smooth dough, 3 to 4 minutes. Add flour as necessary to achieve this consistency, 1 tablespoon at a time (the dough will be slightly sticky). Cover the dough with a clean towel and set in a warm place to rise until doubled in size, about 1 hour.

4. While the dough is rising, make the haupia filling: Combine the cornstarch with ¼ cup of the coconut milk in a small bowl and stir to dissolve. Set aside.

recipe continues on the next page

HAWAIIAN
MALASADAS

continued

5. Combine the remaining 2¼ cups coconut milk and the sugar in a medium saucepan over medium heat and whisk well until the sugar is dissolved, 1 to 2 minutes. Add the salt and the cornstarch slurry and continue whisking until the mixture boils and thickens like pudding, about 5 minutes. Set aside to cool. Fill a large pastry bag with a ½-inch round tip with the cooled filling. Set aside.

6. Once it has risen, punch down the malasada dough and divide into 24 pieces, each about the size of a golf ball. You may have to lightly grease your fingers to prevent the dough from sticking.

7. Place the dough balls on a tray and cover with a clean towel. Set aside in a warm place to rise for another 20 minutes.

8. Heat 3 inches of oil in a large pot set over medium heat. Test the oil by dropping a small piece of dough into it. If it bubbles vigorously and the dough begins to brown, then the oil is ready.

9. Place a wire rack over a sheet pan or line a pan with paper towels. Gently flatten each dough ball into a disk about 3 inches wide and ¼ inch thick and drop it into the hot oil. Don't crowd them in the pan. Fry the malasadas in batches until golden brown on all sides, 1 to 2 minutes per side. Remove with a slotted spoon and place on the wire rack. Allow to cool slightly.

10. Use a sharp paring knife to cut a small, deep slit in the side of a malasada. Insert the tip of the pastry bag and fill the malasada until the haupia comes up to the slit in the doughnut. Repeat with all of the malasadas.

11. To make the topping, mix the cinnamon and sugar together in a small bowl, then sprinkle the malasadas with this mixture.

the malasada's origin

Legend has it that malasadas came about when devout Catholics had to use up the luxury foods in their kitchens, like butter and sugar, in anticipation of the spartan Lenten season ushered in on Ash Wednesday. When Portuguese immigrants came to Hawaii in the nineteenth century to work on the pineapple plantations, they brought the tradition with them, and there it became adapted to local ingredients and customs.

MILLE-FEUILLE
WITH COCONUT PASTRY CREAM

Mille-feuille means "a thousand layers" in French and refers to the flaky puff pastry crust that is the mainstay of this dessert. The Napoleon, which alternates vanilla custard and puff pastry and is iced with sugar icing and a chocolate design, is the most recognizable version of this dish. Here I use coconut pastry cream for the filling and a simple sugar icing flavored with coconut milk and coconut extract. MAKES 6 SERVINGS

pastry

- 1 sheet puff pastry
- 1 tablespoon milk
- 1 tablespoon granulated sugar

filling

- 1 tablespoon cornstarch
- 1 tablespoon water
- ¾ cup coconut milk
- ¼ cup granulated sugar
- ⅛ teaspoon salt
- 2 egg yolks
- 1 teaspoon coconut extract
- ½ teaspoon vanilla extract

icing

- ½ cup confectioners' sugar
- 1 tablespoon coconut milk
- 1 teaspoon water, or more as needed
- ½ teaspoon coconut extract
- 1 ounce bittersweet chocolate

1. To make the pastry, roll out the puff pastry on a large piece of parchment paper to a rectangle that is about 11 by 12 inches. Slice the pastry into three rectangles that are roughly 11 by 4 inches. Refrigerate the pastry for 30 minutes.

2. Preheat the oven to 400°F (200°C).

3. Prick each piece of pastry all over with a fork and then brush with the milk. Sprinkle evenly with the granulated sugar. Bake for 20 minutes, or until golden and puffy. Remove from the oven and cool completely.

4. To make the filling, mix the cornstarch with the water in a small bowl and whisk to combine. Set aside.

5. Combine the coconut milk, granulated sugar, and salt in a medium sauce–pan over medium-low heat. Cook, whisking frequently, until the mixture just starts to simmer around the edges of the pan and the sugar has melted, 3 to 4 minutes.

6. Place the egg yolks in a large bowl and beat to break them apart. Slowly drizzle the hot coconut milk mixture into the eggs, whisking the whole time. When all of the hot milk mixture has been added, return the mixture to the saucepan.

7. Reduce the heat to low and add the cornstarch slurry. Cook, whisking constantly, until the mixture starts to thicken up like pudding, 4 to 5 minutes. Remove from the heat.

8. Mix in the coconut extract and vanilla. Place the pastry cream in a bowl and chill in the refrigerator until it is completely cold, about 2 hours.

9. While the custard is chilling, making the icing: Combine the confectioners' sugar, coconut milk, water, and coconut extract in a large bowl or the bowl of a stand mixer fitted with a balloon whisk attachment. Whisk by hand or with a stand mixer until totally combined into a loose icing. Add more water drop by drop if necessary to achieve this consistency.

10. Place the chocolate in a small microwavable bowl and put in the microwave. Heat on medium or half power for 15-second intervals, not exceeding 2 minutes, until fully melted. Pour the melted chocolate into a small pastry cone and snip off a small hole at the tip.

11. To assemble the milles-feuilles, place one of the puff pastry rectangles on a platter and spread half of the pastry cream evenly on top. Gently place the second layer of puff pastry on top and spread the other half of the pastry cream on that.

12. Lay the last layer of puff pastry on a flat surface and, using an offset spatula, spread the icing evenly on top of it. Using the pastry cone, squeeze lines of chocolate across the short side of the iced pastry about ½ inch apart. Using a toothpick, gently drag the icing perpendicularly across the chocolate lines from one end of the pastry to the other. Do this across the chocolate in ½-inch increments.

13. Gently place the iced pastry layer on top of the other layers of pastry and cream, icing side up. Chill in the refrigerator for 30 minutes before serving.

COCONUT–BANANA
BREAD
PUDDING
WITH RUM-PINEAPPLE
TOPPING

The idea of soaking stale bread in milk and sugar and baking it is the basis for one of the oldest desserts in Western culture: bread pudding. I like to use egg-based bread, like a brioche or challah, because the end product tastes richer. I also make bread pudding in a loaf pan and then turn it out in one piece and slice it, topping with whipped cream and glaze. For a dairy-free version, omit the whipped cream. MAKES 1 LOAF

pudding

- 4 cups 1-inch brioche bread cubes
- 2½ cups coconut milk
- 2 eggs
- 1 very ripe banana, mashed
- 1 teaspoon vanilla extract
- ½ cup granulated sugar
- ½ teaspoon ground cinnamon
- ⅛ teaspoon ground nutmeg

topping

- 2 cups fresh or canned crushed pineapple
- 2 tablespoons light brown sugar
- ¼ cup spiced rum

whipped cream

- 1 cup heavy cream
- ¼ cup confectioners' sugar
- ⅛ teaspoon vanilla extract

1. Preheat the oven to 350°F (180°C). Butter an 8- by 4-inch loaf pan.

2. To make the pudding, place the bread cubes in a large bowl. Pour 1 cup of the coconut milk over the bread cubes and mix well so that all the cubes are moistened. Allow the bread cubes to soak for 10 minutes.

3. Mix remaining 1½ cups coconut milk with the eggs, banana, and vanilla in another large bowl and beat very well. Add the sugar, cinnamon, and nutmeg, and mix well. Add the bread cubes to this mixture and mix thoroughly so the bread is soaked through. Set aside for 10 minutes for the liquid to be absorbed. Mix once again.

4. Pour the bread mixture into the prepared loaf pan and press down firmly so it all fits. Cover the pan with aluminum foil and place in a 9- by 13-inch baking dish. Add enough water to the baking dish to come halfway up the sides of the loaf pan.

recipe continues on the next page

COCONUT-BANANA BREAD PUDDING

continued

5. Bake the pudding for 30 to 40 minutes, or until it is puffed and springs back lightly when touched. Remove from the oven and allow to cool for 10 minutes, then unmold onto a platter.

6. While the pudding is baking, make the pineapple topping: Combine the pineapple, brown sugar, and rum in a medium saucepan over medium-low heat. Stir constantly until the sugar is melted, about 3 minutes. Simmer until the mixture is slightly thickened, 13 to 15 minutes, or until you see holes begin to form on the surface of the mixture. Remove from the heat and set aside to cool for 10 minutes.

7. To make the whipped cream, combine the cream, confectioners' sugar, and vanilla in a large bowl and whip with a whisk until stiff peaks form.

8. Pour the warm pineapple topping over the bread pudding and slice the pudding into ½-inch slices to serve. Top each slice with the whipped cream.

COCONUT TAMALES
(PAIME)

The "sweet tamale" is common throughout the Caribbean, but the ingredients vary. This Trinidadian version features cornmeal, coconut, and pumpkin. Like Toolum (page 186), it's hard to find *paime* (pronounced *pay-mee*) now, although it was once common everywhere. I happen to really love this dessert. It's especially delicious if you pour just a bit of heavy cream over the top when serving. You'll need kitchen twine for this recipe. MAKES 18 TAMALES

¼   cup coconut oil, plus more for brushing the banana leaves

2   tablespoons golden raisins

1½   cups grated fresh or frozen coconut

1½   cups grated calabaza squash or kabocha squash

1¼   cups sugar

2   cups masa harina (corn flour)

1   teaspoon salt

½   teaspoon ground cinnamon

¼   teaspoon ground nutmeg

¾   cup coconut milk, or more as needed

1   teaspoon mixed essence

18   (10- by 10-inch) squares of banana leaf (see note)

Heavy cream for serving

recipe continues on the next page

NOTE: *If using defrosted frozen banana leaves, you may find that they tear easily. Keep the trimmings of your cut banana-leaf squares to patch over any tears before tying up the paime. Alternatively, many cooks layer a square of parchment on top of the banana leaf and then place the paime dough on top of that before folding the whole thing over, which is a good solution, too.*

COCONUT
TAMALES *continued*

1. Heat the coconut oil in a small saucepan over medium-low heat. Add the raisins and fry until they just plump up. Remove from the heat and set aside.

2. Stir together the coconut, pumpkin, and sugar in a large bowl. Add the raisin mixture and mix well.

3. Whisk together the masa harina, salt, cinnamon, and nutmeg in a medium bowl. Add it to the pumpkin mixture and stir well to combine.

4. Combine the coconut milk and mixed essence in a small bowl. Add to the flour mixture, stirring well until you get the consistency of soft play dough. Add more coconut milk or water as needed to achieve this consistency. Divide this dough into 18 pieces.

5. Spread a banana leaf on a flat surface and place one of the dough pieces on it. Fold over the leaf and press down to flatten the dough. Using a rubber spatula, gently push the dough into a 2- by 3-inch rectangle in the middle of the leaf so that it can be covered completely by overlapping one side of the leaf. Fold the banana leaf like you would wrap a package and tie securely with kitchen twine. Repeat with all of the dough and banana leaves.

6. Bring a large pot of water to a boil and gently add the paime. Simmer until the paime feel firm inside their wrappings, 20 to 30 minutes. Remove from the pot.

7. When the leaves are cool enough to handle, unwrap the paime, drizzle with the cream, and serve warm.

paime's different names

African in origin, this dessert is called *paime* in Trinidad but *duckanoo* on other islands — a derivation from its original West African name. Other versions can feature cornmeal alone, or other root vegetables in addition to taro, such as *eddoes* or *batata* (Caribbean sweet potato). The paime is always tied up in a banana leaf similar to the way a tamale is tied up in a corn husk, and steamed. For this reason, another Jamaican name for the dessert is "tie a leaf." In Jamaica, it's also called "blue drawers," perhaps because of the bluish tinge the dessert derives from the taro root that's used in it there.

7
drinks

Coconut's versatility makes it ideal for cocktails and mixed drinks. Once found only in the ubiquitous piña colada in the form of the über-sweet coconut cream, coconut can now be found in waters, sugars, syrups, and liqueurs to round out the bartender's culinary toolkit, adding intense, complex flavors to a wide range of beverages.

This section comprises both cocktails and nonalcoholic drinks, but even those can be spiked as desired. In a similar vein, the liquor can be removed from any of the cocktails to create a "virgin drink," but consider substituting lime juice or plain, unsweetened coconut water for the alcohol in order to balance the flavors.

BITTERS
REVENGE

The best heroes and heroines deliver their revenge sweetly at first and then with a spicy kick at the end. This drink does that as well: the sweet creaminess of coconut liqueur gives way to the warm aromatic complexity of the Angostura bitters and then finishes off with the burn of cayenne pepper. You can find frozen soursop pulp in many supermarkets.

MAKES FOUR 6-OUNCE SERVINGS

1 cup frozen soursop (guanabana) pulp, thawed

1 cup evaporated milk

½ cup aged rum, such as Angostura 1919 (see note)

½ cup coconut cream liqueur, such as Alizé Coco brand

2 tablespoons sweetened cream of coconut, such as Coco Lopez brand

2 tablespoons Angostura bitters

⅛ teaspoon cayenne pepper

2 cups crushed ice

Himalayan pink salt for garnish

Combine the soursop, milk, rum, coconut cream liqueur, coconut cream, bitters, cayenne, and ice in a blender and purée until smooth. Serve in margarita or hurricane glasses. Garnish each drink with a few crystals of salt.

NOTE: *Make sure you use an aged rum that will hold its own against the other ingredients. I prefer Angostura 1919, but you may use any good-quality brown rum you like.*

GLUTEN-FREE

COQUITO

Coquito is the Puerto Rican version of eggnog, made more delicious by — what else? — coconut. Flavored with warm spices and rum, a version of this Christmas-holiday drink is also made in Haiti, where it is called *cremasse*. The recipe makes enough to fill a holiday punch bowl, but feel free to halve the recipe or even quarter it. MAKES 10–12 SERVINGS

2 cups evaporated milk

2 cups cartoned coconut milk, such as So Delicious brand

1 cup sweetened condensed milk

1 cup coconut cream

1 cup premium rum, such as Bacardí Select

½ teaspoon ground cinnamon, plus more for garnish

¼ teaspoon ground nutmeg

4 egg yolks (optional)

1. Combine the evaporated milk, coconut milk, condensed milk, coconut cream, rum, cinnamon, nutmeg, and egg yolks, if using, in a blender. Mix at high speed for 1 to 2 minutes, or until the ingredients are well combined and frothy.

2. Refrigerate immediately until chilled, about 2 hours.

3. Serve in punch glasses, garnished with extra cinnamon.

COCONUT-HIBISCUS
VODKA
MARTINI

Hibiscus drinks and cocktails are quite popular in Central America and much of the Caribbean. They are made by steeping dried roselle (hibiscus) flowers in water with sugar, cinnamon, ginger, and clove to make a tisane. The mild and naturally sweet coconut and the sour and bright hibiscus tisane juxtapose beautifully. You can find dried hibiscus flowers in Caribbean and Middle Eastern markets. MAKES 2 MARTINIS

hibiscus tisane

- 2 cups dried hibiscus flowers, (see note)
- 1 cup granulated sugar
- ½ cinnamon stick
- 1 whole clove
- 3 cups water

martini

- ¼ cup coconut sugar
- 2 cinnamon sticks
- 4 ounces coconut vodka, such as Pearl brand, plus extra for glass rims
- 1 ounce Rose's lime juice
- 4 ice cubes

1. To make the hibiscus tisane, combine the hibiscus, granulated sugar, cinnamon stick, clove, and water in a medium saucepan over medium heat. Bring to a simmer and cook until the liquid is reduced by half, about 20 minutes. Remove from the heat and cover the pan. Allow to steep for 1 hour, then strain and chill. The hibiscus tisane will be more than you need for two martinis, but it's a refreshing drink on its own. It can be stored in an airtight jar in the refrigerator for up to 1 week.

2. To make the martini, place the coconut sugar in a shallow bowl or saucer. Wet a folded, clean paper towel with some of the coconut vodka and wipe around the rims of two large martini glasses. Hold the glasses by the stem and tip the rims into the sugar, twirling to coat evenly. Place the cinnamon sticks in the glasses.

3. Combine the coconut vodka, lime juice, ½ cup hibiscus tisane, and the ice cubes into a cocktail shaker. Shake until the outside of the shaker is cold. Strain the martini into the glasses.

NOTE: *You could also use 4 bags pure hibiscus tea (remove tea from bags and prepare as for the tisane above) or 1½ teaspoons ground hibiscus flowers. If using the ground hibiscus, simmer in 1½ cups water until the sugar is dissolved, 5 to 6 minutes.*

COCOCHINO

I am as much a fan of the American espresso-bar drink as the next person, though I lament how expensive they can be. In addition, I am often frustrated that the only nondairy beverage option is still soy milk when there is perfectly good coconut milk to be had. This Cocochino is made with coconut milk from the carton, which contains a thickener that helps the milk achieve a nice thick froth.   MAKES 2 SERVINGS

1 cup cartoned coconut milk, such as So Delicious brand

1–2 teaspoons sugar

⅛ teaspoon ground ginger

⅛ teaspoon ground nutmeg

2 shots espresso or 1½ cups strong brewed espresso-roasted coffee

Dash of ground cinnamon for garnish (optional)

1. Combine the coconut milk, sugar, ginger, and nutmeg in a medium saucepan over medium-low heat. Whisk well and bring the mixture to just under a boil. Remove from the heat.

2. Add the espresso and pour into a blender. Whir at high speed for 10 to 15 seconds, or until the mixture is frothy, being careful to hold the lid securely.

3. Pour the hot mixture into two coffee mugs and dust with cinnamon, if using.

COCONUT
SWEET TEA

GLUTEN-FREE

DAIRY-FREE

PALEO-FRIENDLY

Sweetened iced tea, or "sweet tea" as it is called in the American South, is a staple summertime beverage. This version uses coconut sugar in place of white sugar and adds coconut water. The result is a sweet — but not overpoweringly so — beverage, with the astringency of the tea softened by the coconut water. MAKES FOUR 8-OUNCE SERVINGS

1 tablespoon loose black tea, such as orange pekoe, or 2 tea bags

4 cups boiling water

½ cup coconut sugar

1 cup coconut water

Ice cubes

Sprigs of fresh mint for garnish

1. Place the tea in a heatproof pitcher or other container and pour the boiling water over it. Mix once and cover. Allow to steep for 2 to 3 minutes, depending on how strong you like your tea. Strain the tea into another container, or remove and discard the tea bags.

2. Add the coconut sugar and mix until it is totally dissolved.

3. Add the coconut water and mix again. Allow the tea mixture to cool completely.

4. Fill four tall glasses with ice, as desired, and pour in the tea mixture. Garnish with mint sprigs and serve.

THAI
ICED TEA

Popular in Thai restaurants in the United States, this spiced-tea drink is most often made with half-and-half or evaporated milk. However, in Thailand, readily available coconut milk is also used for the tea, which may be served hot or cold. Orange flower water can be found in the baking aisle of gourmet grocers or purchased online from King Arthur Flour. MAKES 6-8 SERVINGS

1 tablespoon loose black Ceylon or Assam tea, or 2 tea bags

3 cups boiling water

¼ teaspoon orange flower water

¼ teaspoon vanilla extract

⅛ teaspoon ground cinnamon

⅛ teaspoon ground cloves

½ cup sugar

Crushed ice

2 cups coconut milk, well stirred

1. Place the tea in a heatproof pitcher or other container and pour the boiling water over it. Add the orange flower water, vanilla, cinnamon, and cloves. Mix once and cover. Allow to steep for 4 to 5 minutes.

2. Strain the tea into another container, or remove and discard the tea bags.

3. Add the sugar and mix until it is totally dissolved. Set the mixture aside to cool.

4. Fill eight glasses with ice and add enough tea to fill each glass about two-thirds of the way. Top off each glass with coconut milk. Do not mix. Add a straw and serve. Leftovers will keep in the refrigerator for up to 3 days.

INDIAN-STYLE
MASALA COCONUT TEA

Masala chai is traditionally made with milk and lots of sugar. I've created this version with coconut milk and coconut nectar that, when combined with the spice mix, create a redolent and complex taste experience. The recipe for the masala mix is more than you will use for four servings of tea, but it can be stored in an airtight container for several months and used as needed. MAKES 4 SERVINGS

masala mix

- 1 tablespoon ground ginger
- 1 tablespoon ground cinnamon
- 2 teaspoons ground cardamom
- ½ teaspoon ground cloves
- ½ teaspoon ground nutmeg
- ½ teaspoon freshly ground black pepper

tea

- 3 cups water
- 1 teaspoon masala mix
- 1 cup coconut milk
- 4 tablespoons coconut nectar
- 2 tablespoons black tea

1. To make the masala mix, combine the ginger, cinnamon, cardamom, cloves, nutmeg, and black pepper in a small dish and mix well.

2. To prepare the tea, combine the water with 1 teaspoon of the masala mix in a medium saucepan and bring to a boil over medium heat. Remove from the heat, cover, and allow to steep for 5 minutes.

3. Whisk in the coconut milk and coconut nectar and return the saucepan to the heat. Bring to a boil, whisking until all of the molasses is dissolved. Add the black tea. Remove from the heat, cover, and steep for 3 to 5 minutes, depending how strong you like your tea.

4. Strain into four mugs. Serve hot.

VARIATION: CAFFEINE-FREE MASALA

The masala mix is also delicious whisked into heated coconut milk, with a dash of vanilla, for a caffeine-free drink. Use about ½ teaspoon per cup of milk.

the flavors of masala chai

Masala chai, or "spiced tea" with plenty of milk, is a staple beverage for much of the Indian subcontinent. Transported to the West under the redundant moniker "chai tea" (*chai* is the Indian word for tea), this hot beverage features spices like cinnamon, cardamom, ginger, nutmeg, clove, and pepper for a deliciously warming flavor profile. The amounts of the various spices can be adjusted to suit your tastes — there is no "wrong" mix of masala for tea.

COCONUT-CHOCOLATE
MILK SHAKE

The old-school precursors to the smoothie, milk shakes are decadent treats that bring to mind the nostalgia of the soda fountain. This modern-day version combines coconut ice cream (homemade or purchased) with the classic Fox's U-bet chocolate syrup that would have been in the toolkit of any soda jerk of yore. Of course, chocolate aficionados might want to substitute a higher-end brand of syrup, and that's more than fine, too. MAKES 4 SERVINGS

3 scoops coconut ice cream (store-bought or from the recipe on page 229)

½ cup unsweetened cartoned coconut milk, such as So Delicious brand

¼ cup chocolate syrup, such as Fox's U-bet

Pinch of sea salt for garnish (optional)

Whipped cream for garnish

Maraschino cherry for garnish

1. Combine the ice cream, coconut milk, and chocolate syrup in a blender and process until smooth and thick, about 1 minute.

2. Pour the milk shake into four glasses and garnish each with a small amount of sea salt (if using), whipped cream, and a maraschino cherry. Serve.

VERY BERRY
FIBER-RICH
SMOOTHIE

Among coconut's many health properties, fiber is a number one benefit. The recommended dietary allowance (RDA) for fiber for an adult is 25 grams. One cup of coconut meat provides more than a third of that amount, and 3 tablespoons of flaxseed meal offers about a quarter of your fiber RDA. This smoothie is so fiber-dense that you'll very nearly reach your daily quota with one small (4-ounce) glass. MAKES 4 SERVINGS

1½ cups coconut milk

½ cup dried unsweetened shredded coconut

½ cup fresh blackberries

½ cup fresh raspberries

¼ cup ground flaxseed meal

¼ teaspoon ground cardamom

Combine the coconut milk, shredded coconut, blackberries, raspberries, flaxseed meal, and cardamom in a blender and purée until smooth. Divide among four glasses. Serve cold.

COCONUT-PINEAPPLE
SMOOTHIE

If you like piña coladas, you'll love this smoothie. It has all the romance of the classic coconut-pineapple duet without any of the liquor. Instead, the punch from this drink comes from the protein powder that turns it from a deliciously decadent treat into a powerful health drink.

MAKES 4 SERVINGS

2	cups vanilla-flavored coconut milk yogurt
1	cup frozen pineapple chunks
½	cup water
3	tablespoons gluten-free protein powder such as whey or hemp seed
1	tablespoon honey or coconut nectar
1	teaspoon vanilla extract

Combine the yogurt, pineapple, water, protein powder, honey, and vanilla in a blender and purée until smooth. Divide among four glasses. Serve cold.

PROTEIN-PACKED
SMOOTHIE

Protein keeps us feeling full and satisfied and is often sorely lacking in simple smoothie recipes. This protein-packed shake is great for breakfast on the go, and it is sweet enough to entice even the little ones.   MAKES 4 SERVINGS

2	cups coconut milk
¼	cup coconut manna
¼	cup peanut butter
¼	cup chocolate-flavored gluten-free protein powder
1	teaspoon unsweetened cocoa powder
1	teaspoon vanilla extract

Combine the coconut milk, coconut manna, peanut butter, protein powder, cocoa powder, and vanilla in a high-powered blender and purée until smooth. Divide among four glasses. Serve cold.

glossary

AJÍ DULCE. A small sweet pepper closely resembling a Scotch bonnet (habanero) but without the heat. Often called a "seasoning" pepper, it is closest in flavor to pimiento or hot paprika.

CALABAZA. A variety of pumpkin grown in the Caribbean and Latin America with yellow or green skin and sweet flesh.

CULANTRO (RECAO). This relative of cilantro has a similar taste to that herb but a totally different appearance, with long oval leaves and sharp teeth around the edges. Also called *shadon beni (chandon benet)* in parts of the Caribbean, the herb is most often associated with Mexico.

CURRY LEAF. A tropical leaf from the curry tree, it grows in South Asia and is added to curry spice mixtures as well as directly to various dishes for flavor. It is sold fresh on the stem in small quantities, as it loses its pungency when it dries out.

DENDÊ. The oil of the red palm nut, this African oil is also used prodigiously in Brazil and is often available as a gourmet oil in Western supermarkets.

DRIED SHRIMP. Used in a variety of dishes from Southeast Asia to South America, these shrimp are small and used as flavoring in soups and stews. Occasionally dried shrimp are ground into a powder for seasoning.

FERMENTED SHRIMP PASTE. A Southeast Asian flavoring agent made from fermented shrimp that is ground and mixed with salt.

GREEN SEASONING. A mixed green herb and spice paste that is used in stews and soups throughout the Caribbean.

GUANABANA (SOURSOP). A tropical fruit with white flesh and naturally sweet-tart flavor, it is native to Central America and the Caribbean and is in the same family as cherimoya.

HARISSA. This North African hot chile paste comprises smoked hot peppers and a variety of warm spices like coriander, cumin, and caraway in a ratio that depends on the region. Harissa usually also has garlic and is processed with olive oil or other oil.

KAFFIR LIME. Kaffir lime trees are native to southern Asia. The lime is aromatic with a bumpy green skin. The leaves are also aromatic and are often used in rice dishes, soups, stews, and confections for a light citrus flavor and aroma.

MALAGUETA CHILE. An extremely hot pepper, it originated in Mozambique and traveled to Portugal and Brazil with African slaves. It is used most often in the cuisine of Bahia in Brazil.

MALDIVE FISH FLAKES. These are dried flakes of a variety of bonito tuna found in the region of the Maldives. They are used as a flavoring in curries and stews.

MASA HARINA. This finely ground corn flour is used in tamales.

MIXED ESSENCE. This Caribbean baking extract combines artificial almond, orange, and pear flavoring to mimic an original extract made by soaking tonka beans in rum.

NAM PLA OR PATIS. This is a fish sauce used in Southeast Asia. *Nam pla* is the Thai name and *patis* the Filipino version.

SEVILLE ORANGE JUICE. A bitter juice, it is extracted from Seville oranges.

SHICHIMI TOGARASHI. A Japanese spicy-aromatic powdered seasoning, it is used in broths and soups.

SUMAC. A sour red seasoning powder made from dried sumac berries, it is most often used in Middle Eastern dishes.

SWEET RICE FLOUR. A rice flour made from glutinous rice, it is available in Asian markets.

TAHINI. A paste made from ground sesame seeds, it is commonly used throughout the Middle East.

TAMARIND SYRUP. This concentrated syrup is made from boiling down tamarind pod pulp with white sugar.

URAD DAL. A bean grown in the Indian subcontinent, it is also called black lentil or black gram. It is used for stews and soups and ground for use as a dough for South Indian crêpes called *dosa* and the crispy Indian wafers called *papads* that are often served as an appetizer in Indian restaurants.

YUCCA (CASSAVA). A tuber commonly used in Africa and the Caribbean, yucca is the basis for tapioca starch.

recipes by dietary type

gluten-free recipes

dairy-free recipes

paleo-friendly recipes

additional photography credits

index

Page numbers in *italic* indicate photos.

SAVOR THE FLAVORS
WITH MORE STOREY BOOKS

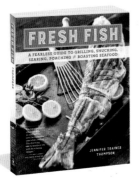

by Jennifer Trainer Thompson
COOK THE DAY'S CATCH WITH CONFIDENCE!
From Bay Scallop Ceviche to Wild Striped Bass with Pistachio Crust, these 175 recipes bring out the best flavors in seafood and accompanying dishes.

by Laurey Masterton
CELEBRATE THE FLAVORS OF HONEY
with more than 80 seasonal recipes that focus on what's fresh each month. With different varieties of honey, such as sage or avocado, try recipes like Pork Tenderloin with Orange Blossom Honey Mustard or Baked Acorn Squash.

by Jennifer Trainer Thompson
FEEL THE BURN BY MAKING YOUR OWN HOT SAUCE! Treat your taste buds to a delicious wallop with 32 recipes for creating your own signature blends, plus 60 more recipes for cooking with homemade or commercial versions.

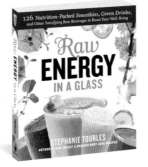

by Stephanie Tourles
RAISE A GLASS TO LONGEVITY!
Boost your health and energy using just a standard blender and these 126 super-nutritious, super-delicious recipes for smoothies, fruity frappés, vegan shakes, power shots, mocktails, and more.